Scaling Pyramids

Leadership doesn't start at the top—it starts with you.

Scaling Pyramids: Leadership Lessons from a Mid-Level Bureaucrat is an honest, engaging, and research-informed exploration of what it means to lead from the bottom and middle of an organization—especially within complex systems that aren't always built for innovation, agility, or humanity.

Drawing on more than 25 years of experience as a federal law enforcement officer, diplomat, educator, and public servant, author Christopher Stitt brings a rare combination of street-level credibility and scholarly insight to the leadership conversation. Throughout the book, he weaves together personal stories from his global assignments with contemporary leadership research from behavioral science, organizational psychology, and decision-making theory.

The result is a practical and thought-provoking field guide for those who are tired of waiting for permission to lead—and ready to make a difference right where they are.

In these pages, you'll find lessons on how to influence up, down, and across your organization. You'll learn how to build trust, coach others, think strategically, and maintain your integrity even when politics or process get in the way. You'll discover why the middle of the organizational pyramid is not a waiting room for the next promotion—it's the center of gravity where culture, performance, and credibility are either built or broken.

Whether you're managing teams in a government agency, navigating the corporate hierarchy, or trying to make change from within a large institution, *Scaling Pyramids* offers you a road map grounded in both lived experience and real evidence. With a voice that is both candid and deeply practical, Stitt reminds us that leadership isn't about rank—it's about showing up, stepping up, and speaking up in the moments that matter.

If you've ever felt overlooked, underutilized, or underestimated in your role, this book is for you.

It's time to lead. Not someday—now.

Security, Audit and Leadership Series

Series Editor: Dan Swanson, Dan Swanson and Associates, Ltd., Winnipeg, Manitoba, Canada.

The scope and mandate for internal audit continues to evolve each year, as does the complexity of the business environment and speed of the changing risk landscape in which it must operate. The fundamental goal of this exciting series is to produce leading-edge books on critical subjects facing security and audit executives and practitioners. Key topics addressed include Leadership, Cybersecurity, Security Leadership, Privacy, Strategic Risk Management, Auditing IT, Audit Management and Leadership, and Operational Auditing.

Members, Methods, and Measures: *Unlocking the Secrets of IT Leadership*
By Thomas E. Armstrong

Philosophy.exe: *The Techno-Philosophical Toolkit for Modern Minds*
By Matthias Muhlert

Guardians of the Digital Age: *Securing the Future*
By Elçin Biren

Ironwill 360° Leadership: *A Blueprint for Level 5 Unicorn Leadership*
By Douglas P. Pflug

Behavioral Insights in Cybersecurity: *A Guide to Digital Human Factors*
By Dustin S. Sachs

Integrated Assurance: *Unified Risk Strategy*
By Patrick Hayes

Preparing for Sustainability Audits: *A Practical Guide for IT Sector*
By Mahsa Fidanboy

Scaling Pyramids: *Leadership Lessons from a Mid-Level Bureaucrat*
By Christopher Stitt

In "Scaling Pyramids," Chris offers a candid and insightful exploration of the often-misunderstood world of bureaucracy. As his friend, I've had the privilege of witnessing his dedication and thoughtful approach to leadership. This book is a testament to his journey through the "Department of Pyramids," where he navigated the complexities of hierarchical structures while fostering a culture of accountability and efficiency.

Chris's experiences, from his early days as an entry-level employee to his mid-level management roles, are filled with valuable lessons on leadership and personal growth. He shares practical advice on understanding your values, managing your strengths and weaknesses, and the importance of self-care. His stories about leading others are equally compelling, offering strategies for building alliances, motivating employees, and developing leadership character.

What sets this book apart is Chris's ability to relate his experiences to broader organizational principles. Whether you're an entry-level employee or a mid-level manager, you'll find his insights on communicating vision, navigating the pyramid, and leveraging project teams incredibly useful. Chris's approach to leadership is both practical and inspiring, making this book a must-read for anyone in a leadership role, and those endeavoring to someday be.

Nick Anderson, *CEO OneAccord*

In my executive coaching work, I frequently encounter new professionals trying to understand how to manage teams and navigate a bureaucracy. Too often leadership books target senior level leaders managing down, but there is not enough support for the entry- or mid-level manager trying to manage up. In Scaling Pyramids, Chris dives into this conundrum with a practical guide containing real life lessons on how to navigate an organization and maximize influence.

Grounding his readers in tried and tested values, Chris balances his actual experience in crisis management with immediately applicable lessons on how to gain traction with fresh ideas, deal with the Alpha in an office, and stand out from the group while keeping the team in front. Whether it's responding to 9/11 while overseas or revamping an entirely new Department as a low level manager, Chris guides his readers with a fresh approach in how to apply leadership principles he has personally learned regardless of the complexity of the situation. Professionals will come away better equipped to manage their teams, navigate their bureaucracies, and find upward success while holding true to their values. A book not to be missed.

Stephanie Mikulasek, *ServantEDGE Coaching*
Former U.S. Diplomat

"I am a mid-level bureaucrat." Christopher Stitt begins this book Scaling Pyramids with a startling statement given the socio-political environment we live in. What can I possibly learn from being stuck in the swamp? But what he discovers is that this is every man's journey, every organization's journey. And there is a way to navigate this human organizational construct that delivers purpose, dignity, and value.

Ron Worman, *The Sage Group*®

Chris' portrayal of his lived experience as a mid-level government bureaucrat is a masterclass in navigating leadership challenges in both government and corporate settings. Leaders in the industry will identify with the challenges he describes and will take note of the best practices and solutions. This book is a simple to digest and good read for anyone embarking on their first leadership position in government or the private sector.

Brian Cooke, *DSS Special Agent – Retired,*
Fortune 25 company security leader,
Security & Intelligence

Who knew you could learn about leadership from a long-time mid-level government employee? You can when he's Christopher Stitt, a self-described bureaucrat who navigated his way to leadership – in practice and influence if not in title – during an impressive career at the Department of State.

To generalize his experiences, Stitt uses the playful "Department of Pyramids" as a stand-in for his actual employer. He mines his globetrotting governmental career to provide unexpected insights into leadership, tying in lessons from his youth as an Eagle Scout and a Dungeons & Dragons devotee. Nuggets of wisdom emerge from such far-flung posts in Central America and Africa.

With wit and warmth, Chris describes his journey and leaves helpful breadcrumbs for fellow bureaucrats with leadership aspirations. It's a compelling read from a charmingly earnest guide.

Michael Gips, *Managing Director for ESRM at Kroll*
Former Chief Knowledge Officer at ASIS International
#1 Globally Ranked thought leader in security

Scaling Pyramids

Leadership Lessons from a Mid-Level Bureaucrat

Christopher Stitt

CRC Press
Taylor & Francis Group
Boca Raton London New York

CRC Press is an imprint of the
Taylor & Francis Group, an **informa** business

Designed cover image: Shutterstock Image ID 96622405

First edition published 2026
by CRC Press
2385 NW Executive Center Drive, Suite 320, Boca Raton FL 33431

and by CRC Press
4 Park Square, Milton Park, Abingdon, Oxon, OX14 4RN

CRC Press is an imprint of Taylor & Francis Group, LLC

© 2026 Christopher Stitt

ISBN: 978-1-041-08867-7 (hbk)
ISBN: 978-1-041-09506-4 (pbk)
ISBN: 978-1-003-65045-4 (ebk)

DOI: 10.1201/9781003650454

Typeset in Sabon
by Newgen Publishing UK

To my wife, Denise, and our children, for all of your love and support on this continuing journey.

Contents

Foreword

In the labyrinthine corridors of bureaucracy, where progress often seems sluggish and the path forward obscured, few individuals possess the acumen not only to navigate but also to thrive. Chris Stitt is one such individual. His new book, *Scaling Pyramids: Leadership Lessons from a Mid-Level Bureaucrat*, offers a rare and invaluable perspective on leadership within complex government and corporate organizations.

I have had the privilege of knowing Chris for several years, and in that time, I have witnessed his unwavering commitment to personal and professional growth. A graduate of the Institute of Presilience, Chris embodies the principles of resilience, risk intelligence, and agility. His approach to leadership is not merely theoretical; it is deeply rooted in lived experience and a genuine empathy for those he leads.

What sets Chris apart is his nuanced understanding of people. He does not view leadership as a hierarchical imposition but as a collaborative endeavor that recognizes the intrinsic value of each individual. This empathy, combined with his strategic foresight, allows him to inspire and lead effectively, even in the most challenging environments.

Scaling Pyramids is not just a guide for those early in their careers; it is an invaluable resource for leaders at all levels. Chris delves into the intricacies of bureaucratic systems, offering insights that are both practical and profound. He draws from his own experiences, sharing both successes and setbacks, providing readers with a balanced perspective that is often lacking in traditional leadership literature.

One of the book's most commendable aspects is its incorporation of models, tools, and ideas from global leaders. Chris has synthesized these diverse perspectives, presenting them in a manner that is accessible and actionable. The inclusion of anecdotes further enriches the narrative, offering readers concrete examples of how these concepts play out in real-world scenarios.

This book serves as a playbook for those entering and navigating large organizations. The structure of the book focuses on the progressive importance of self-leadership, leading others, and finally leading organizations, regardless of rank or title. It provides strategies for getting things done while maintaining integrity and fostering positive relationships. Chris's ability to distill complex concepts into actionable steps makes this work indispensable for anyone aiming to lead with efficacy and empathy.

In closing, I have known Chris to be a perpetual learner and teacher. His dedication to personal development and his passion for sharing knowledge are evident in every page of this book. *Scaling Pyramids* is more than just a leadership manual; it is a reflection of Chris's journey and his commitment to empowering others to succeed in the intricate world of bureaucracy.

Dr. Gavriel (Gav) Schneider
FGIA, FISRM, FARPI, CPP, RPP, CCRO
Creator of the Presilience Approach
CEO, Risk 2 Solution Group

Preface

Leadership. It is a big topic with a lot already written about it and more coming every day. One of the reasons I like the topic is that it is so dynamic and so important.

We live in a world that is increasingly volatile, uncertain, complex, ambiguous, and digitized. There is a lot of research into these concepts and the fact that they require leadership, as opposed to simply management. If complex or "wicked" problems could be solved through simply managing them, we would not have any complex or wicked problems. If we had all the information we needed and could easily trace a given problem to its source, clearly identifying the cause and remedy to correct it, we could manage everything without a need for leadership.

But the world, and the workforce, is not that simple. It requires people who can look at a situation, with incomplete information and uncertainty about outcomes, and say, "here is what needs to be done," and get people to buy in and follow them through the trials of the solution.

PROGRAMS REQUIRE MANAGEMENT. PEOPLE NEED LEADERSHIP

Are leaders born or made? Some people have a natural charisma that causes people to follow them; others have a natural intelligence that makes them great problem solvers. The best leaders couple this with a growth mindset of active learning in a variety of domains. Again, there is a lot of research into the neuroscience and psychology of critical thinking, decision-making, and emotional intelligence. In my experience, the best leaders are the ones who are lifelong students of leadership. They constantly learn, reflect, and adjust their skills and styles to meet the moment.

SO WHY THIS BOOK AND WHO IS IT FOR?

I originally started this book as a cathartic exercise in response to a couple of really poor managers. They believed themselves to be leaders, but more people fled than were attracted to them. As I reflected on my experiences with them, I also reflected on the best managers and leaders I had worked with and the evolution of my own leadership style. Where I felt it was appropriate, I have incorporated contemporary research and the voices of top leadership experts.

The lessons that I have presented throughout this book are not just meant for you, they are also meant for me.

I have intentionally focused this book on the first half of my career. There are a couple of reasons for this, namely, the population of readers I am hoping to reach and influence, and because this time is so foundational in the development of leadership skills and style. The habits you build in the early part of your career tend to stick with you throughout, so building good habits is important.

My goal is to help:

- People who are about to or have recently entered the workforce;
- People who have been in a couple of years and are feeling ready to advance in their careers;
- People who are hoping to continue advancing, but are feeling stuck.

Following the advice in this book will not guarantee promotions and advancement in your organization. Reading this book will give you some things to reflect on in your own leadership journey as you navigate your own bureaucracy.

MY BUREAUCRACY AND JOURNEY...

I spent more almost 30 years in law enforcement and security, the vast majority of which was with the US Department of State's Diplomatic Security Service. Often referred to as DS or DSS, Diplomatic Security is a bit unusual. First of all, as a Special Agent, I was a member of the Foreign Service. This means a couple of things: I rotated assignments regularly, a new office or even country every one to three years. It also means I had the opportunity to learn from a lot of different cultures and leadership styles. Agents in DS are given a lot of responsibility very quickly, be it holding leadership positions on protective details for major foreign leaders, coordinating investigations into federal crimes, or managing programs that involve dozens or even hundreds of people. I experienced all of this, and more, within my first five years on the job. And that is typical.

Also, Diplomatic Security is what is now referred to in the corporate world as a "matrixed organization." When overseas, our reporting chains went up through the ambassador, but we also had reporting and coordination responsibilities for a variety of offices in DS headquarters in the Washington, DC, area.

I started my career as an entry-level Special Agent assigned to the New York Field Office, one of the largest in DS. After less than a year, I was off to training for my first overseas assignment, and then throughout my career I rotated between assignments in the US and abroad, living overseas for about 11 of my 26 years in service. I have lived in five countries outside the United States (including in Africa, Central America, and the Middle East) and worked in or visited a total of about 45. I finished my career as a Deputy Regional Director in International Programs, providing guidance and oversight to the embassy and consulate security offices throughout the Americas and Caribbean.

Much like the military, the Foreign Service is rank-in-person, not rank-in-position. This means that you are evaluated for promotion based on your perceived readiness, as assessed through the annual employee evaluation process, to take on responsibilities at the next highest level. Once you are promoted, you are eligible to bid on assignments at the next highest level. There may be possibilities to obtain "stretch" assignments, one grade above your current level, but that does not necessarily mean you will get promoted to that level (unlike the civil service, when serving in a position for a year causes you to be promoted to the grade of the position). You can also end up in a "down-stretch" position, particularly if your promotion comes through after your assignment has been made. This does not mean you will be demoted or not get your promotion. Frankly, this happened to me toward the end of my career, but since I was now overgraded for my position, the office leadership found ways to give me additional responsibilities commensurate with my grade rather than simply my position. Good leadership.

For reference, the Foreign Service grade system goes in the opposite direction of the military. I started as an FS-06 (equivalent to a second lieutenant) and retired as an FS-01 (equivalent to a colonel).

While I have provided the above explanation to give you context and to help you understand some of the things that shape my perspective, for the purpose of this book, who I am and who I worked for does not really matter. Yes, I draw on anecdotes from my career to illustrate the points I am trying to make, but ultimately, what is important for you, the reader, to understand is that I worked in a bureaucracy. In fact, one of the biggest around, the US federal government. But, as I get into in the introduction, almost every organization, public, private, government, or corporate, is a bureaucracy, or at least has bureaucratic attributes. Learning to navigate and lead in this environment will be crucial for success: for you, your teams, and your organizations.

So let's go. Follow me.

Acknowledgments

Writing a book develops its own bureaucracy and I give thanks to mine for this project. For the initial inspiration, thanks to those leaders and managers, both good and bad, who provided the examples that are contained herein and many more I experienced.

To Steve Antoine, who found an early copy of the draft and encouraged me to complete it. He is also the model of a personally oriented, continuously learning leader.

To Michael Gips, who was amused by the concept and connected me with Dan Swanson, the series editor at CRC Press. Mike continued to encourage and support me through the process and is an amazing friend and mentor.

To Dan Swanson, Gabriella Williams, and the team at Taylor & Francis who helped me navigate the process of turning the rough manuscript into this published volume. I appreciate your guidance and feedback.

As I scaled this pyramid of book writing, I had a handful of pre-readers who provided their feedback, thoughts, and suggested edits to make the book better. Michael Gips, Dr. Gav Schneider, Stephanie Mikulasek, and Brian Cooke, I am in your debt for the care and time you took to help me.

While I dedicated this book to my wife, Denise, and our children, I want to give them a special acknowledgment here for sticking with me on my evolving leadership journey including the highs and lows, the triumphs and frustrations. Also, for bearing with me as I took time away from our family vacations and other events to work on the draft and revisions. I love you all. So much.

To my parents, friends, and mentors, some of whom I mention in the book and others I do not, thank you for being role models and inspirations and helping to shape me into the leader I am today. Special thanks to Jack and Margaret Stitt, Jason Stitt, Michael Liderbach, Josh Rakow, Bill Thomas, Mark Lewis, Jim Gayhart, Julie Cabus, Charlie Brandeis, Douglas Kinney, Barry Heyman, Anson Garlington, Pastor Glenn Hershberger, Ron Worman, Dr. Rob McKenna and Dr. Daniel Hallack and the team at WiLD Leaders, and Lee Oughton, Tim Wenzel, and the folks I have met through

The Kindness Games. There are many others, and I ask your grace and forgiveness if I have not included you in this list.

For those that took the time to review and provide the advance praise contained in the front of the book, thank you. Your kindness and words inspire me to keep going. Your unique viewpoints as you read the manuscript affirm that this book is applicable to all who are scaling their own pyramids: government, corporate, or other.

Finally, thank YOU, the reader for taking the time to review the lessons, reflect on them, and apply them in your own journeys through the pyramids.

About the author

Christopher Stitt is a seasoned security and leadership professional with over 25 years of experience in risk management, organizational development, and public service. A former US Diplomatic Security Service Supervisory Special Agent, Stitt has led global teams across high-threat environments and complex bureaucracies—ranging from embassies and crisis zones to federal headquarters and academic institutions.

Known for his practical, principle-driven leadership style, Stitt has spent his career helping people and organizations navigate risk, build resilience, and develop high-performing cultures. He is the founder and CEO of CrisisLead, LLC, and a respected educator, speaker, mentor, and coach. Stitt holds multiple leadership, risk, and emergency management certifications and teaches homeland security courses as an adjunct faculty member at George Mason University.

Scaling Pyramids aims to share the hard-earned lessons of leading well from the middle, influencing upward, and shaping organizations from within. He has previously published a chapter in the book *The Kindness Games: How a Single Post Changed Our Mindset about Community*, along with multiple articles and blog posts for security and leadership publications. He is a frequent podcast guest and speaker at conferences and corporate events.

Introduction

As I mentioned in the preface, who I am is not important. Nor is who I worked for. The key point is that I spent several years as a mid-level bureaucrat in a US government agency. Realizing I was a mid-level bureaucrat was something of a shock and a surprise. I was sitting at my desk one day and out of the blue, it hit me, "I am a mid-level bureaucrat." This term carries a lot of baggage, most of it bad. I suppose I could have stuck with, "I am a mid-level manager," and maybe felt better about myself, but frankly, I worked in a bureaucracy.

As I toyed with the concept in my head, it dawned on me what it really means to be a mid-level bureaucrat. Like I said, I started thinking of myself as a mid-level manager. I began in an entry-level position and I had been promoted a couple of times to reach the upper mid-level of my agency. It was a position of responsibility. At the time this revelation hit me, I had several people that I supervised directly and about 200 others that I supervised indirectly. I oversaw the operations of an office with an annual budget approaching two million dollars. On paper, and in reality, it sounds like I was pretty successful, and really, I feel pretty successful.

Then I started to think about where I was working, not physically where, but the type of organization. And that is when it hit me: I was not just a mid-level manager, I was a mid-level bureaucrat.

Bureaucracy has many negative connotations these days. What comes to mind when you hear the term? I can guess a lot of things that popped into your head: slow, inefficient, bulky, archaic, government, institution. The DMV, the IRS, Social Security, and the Department of Veterans Affairs. We have all heard horror stories of standing in line for hours on end, or waiting months for services, and then there is the stereotypical government employee sitting across the counter, just another cog in the uncaring machine.

The truth is that bureaucracy is organization and efficiency. Without it, we would be lost. According to Bert Rockman in his article on Britannica. com, bureaucracy is a "specific form of organization defined by complexity, division of labour, permanence, professional management, hierarchical coordination and control, strict chain of command, and legal authority" (Rockman, 2025).

Rockman explores the work of German sociologist Max Weber, who "observed that the advantage of bureaucracy was that it was the most technically proficient form of organization, possessing specialized expertise, certainty, continuity, and unity" (Rockman, 2025).

Rockman ultimately summarizes bureaucracy this way: "The most basic elements of pure bureaucratic organization are its emphasis on procedural regularity, a hierarchical system of accountability and responsibility, specialization of function, continuity, a legal-rational basis, and fundamental conservatism" (Rockman, 2025). Bureaucracy is what makes our modern systems of government, business, and finance function.

Looking back at my own experience, a great example of this occurred to me as I was completing some paperwork for the Boy Scouts. As I will discuss in Part 1, I was a Boy Scout growing up and now that I am an adult, I have given back by volunteering my time with local troops. So, as I was filling out some paperwork and talking on the phone with one of the Scouting professionals at the Boy Scouts of America headquarters in Texas, I suddenly had a flash of insight into the bureaucracy of the Boy Scouts.

As a Scout, I earned merit badges and ranks, all the way through Eagle Scout, but I never saw all of the work happens after the meetings to track those accomplishments and officially catalog them. Now, on the adult side, as I worked to make sure all of the paperwork was lined up as two boys in the troop finished the last requirements for their own Eagle Scout Awards, it hit me: Boy Scouts of America is a bureaucracy. This is a good thing, heck, even a great thing. It is the organization and standardization of information that gives it credibility. They do not simply make up the details; the details are laboriously recorded, in an attributable fashion, with signatures to ensure accountability.

To me, that is what is best about bureaucracy. While it has been stereotyped and maligned over the years, at its core, the definition of bureaucracy is a hierarchical organization that ensures attribution and accountability. The goal of bureaucracy is efficiency, much to the chagrin of the pundits, and a good bureaucracy is always on the lookout to adopt more efficient methodologies and streamline operations. My experience with the bureaucracy of the Boy Scouts brought this home to me, and suddenly I realized, "I am a bureaucrat too."

As I continued to reflect on what this meant, I started to think about how I got here. As I mentioned, I was not just a bureaucrat, I was a mid-level bureaucrat. I led people and managed programs. I had moved up in my organization with hopes to continue forward. Along the way, I learned a lot of things, some good, others ... yeah, not so much. The nature of the government agency I worked for kept me moving; I rotated jobs every two to three years. This means I've had a lot of examples to draw on and learn from.

Speaking of this, let me digress for a moment and talk about my career path. As I said earlier, the agency I worked for is not important. The lessons I learned and that I share in this book are just as easily applied to any bureaucracy, but without some context, the rest of this book will be awfully confusing to you, the reader. So, in order to protect the innocent, and sometimes the guilty, most of the names in this book have been changed.

While I mentioned in the preface that I spent most of my career in the Department of State, for the sake of argument, let's call the agency where I worked the US Department of Pyramids. Like all good government departments, we have a secretary of pyramids, a deputy secretary of pyramids, and a couple of undersecretaries, each of whom has assistant secretaries, who oversees various regional or functional affairs related to pyramids. This continues down to the base level of the workers who actually do the frontline work. The reason I choose to refer to my agency as the "Department of Pyramids" is because bureaucracies are generally shaped like pyramids.

At the top is the secretary or chief executive officer or president of the organization/business/agency. Below the CEO is a layer of vice presidents, deputies, undersecretaries, and so forth. In reality, most organizations are made up of pyramids within pyramids that form reporting chains. These reporting chains are useful because they allow information to filter up and be vetted at each level so that only the most important information reaches the top. These reporting chains are also useful as action requirements can be passed down to the appropriate levels, with oversight to ensure the actions are taken.

Figure 0.1 is a graphic depiction of this for the government side, and Figure 0.2 is a graphic depiction of how this typically aligns on the corporate side.

The Department of Pyramids Structure

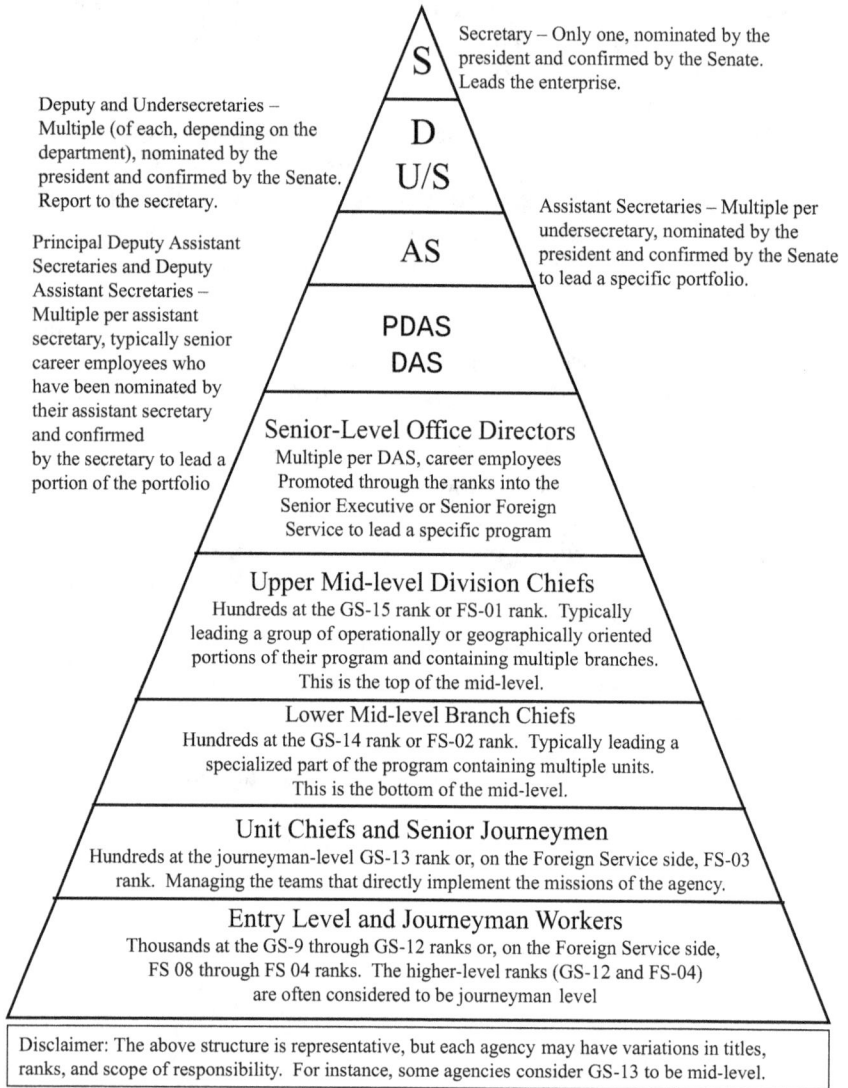

Secretary – Only one, nominated by the president and confirmed by the Senate. Leads the enterprise.

S

Deputy and Undersecretaries – Multiple (of each, depending on the department), nominated by the president and confirmed by the Senate. Report to the secretary.

D

U/S

Assistant Secretaries – Multiple per undersecretary, nominated by the president and confirmed by the Senate to lead a specific portfolio.

AS

Principal Deputy Assistant Secretaries and Deputy Assistant Secretaries – Multiple per assistant secretary, typically senior career employees who have been nominated by their assistant secretary and confirmed by the secretary to lead a portion of the portfolio

PDAS
DAS

Senior-Level Office Directors
Multiple per DAS, career employees Promoted through the ranks into the Senior Executive or Senior Foreign Service to lead a specific program

Upper Mid-level Division Chiefs
Hundreds at the GS-15 rank or FS-01 rank. Typically leading a group of operationally or geographically oriented portions of their program and containing multiple branches. This is the top of the mid-level.

Lower Mid-level Branch Chiefs
Hundreds at the GS-14 rank or FS-02 rank. Typically leading a specialized part of the program containing multiple units. This is the bottom of the mid-level.

Unit Chiefs and Senior Journeymen
Hundreds at the journeyman-level GS-13 rank or, on the Foreign Service side, FS-03 rank. Managing the teams that directly implement the missions of the agency.

Entry Level and Journeyman Workers
Thousands at the GS-9 through GS-12 ranks or, on the Foreign Service side, FS 08 through FS 04 ranks. The higher-level ranks (GS-12 and FS-04) are often considered to be journeyman level

Disclaimer: The above structure is representative, but each agency may have variations in titles, ranks, and scope of responsibility. For instance, some agencies consider GS-13 to be mid-level.

Figure 0.1 A graphical representation of a typical government bureaucratic pyramid, with descriptions of each level of management.

Typical Corporate Pyramid Structure

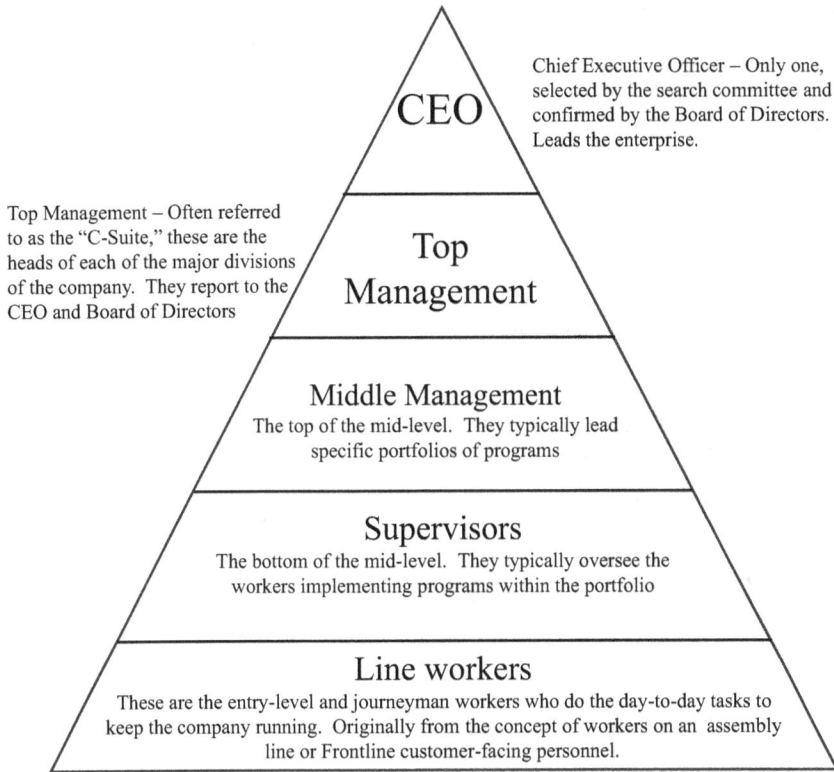

CEO

Chief Executive Officer – Only one, selected by the search committee and confirmed by the Board of Directors. Leads the enterprise.

Top Management – Often referred to as the "C-Suite," these are the heads of each of the major divisions of the company. They report to the CEO and Board of Directors

Top Management

Middle Management
The top of the mid-level. They typically lead specific portfolios of programs

Supervisors
The bottom of the mid-level. They typically oversee the workers implementing programs within the portfolio

Line workers
These are the entry-level and journeyman workers who do the day-to-day tasks to keep the company running. Originally from the concept of workers on an assembly line or Frontline customer-facing personnel.

Disclaimer: the above structure is representative, but there are significant variations. In fact, multinational conglomerates often have a complicated structure similar to the Department of Pyramids structure on the previous page. On the other hand, small businesses often roll all of the levels into one or two.

Figure 0.2 A graphical representation of a typical corporate pyramid, with descriptions of each level of management.

I know that there is a trend to "flatten" organizations, which can be incredibly useful because in the pyramid-within-pyramid reporting chains, there is a chance that great ideas get squashed before they make it up to a level where they can be decided upon and implemented. Some really old-school bureaucracies are taking a hybrid approach. My own agency still has the formal, bureaucratic, pyramid-within-pyramid reporting chains, but they have also implemented some shortcuts into the system for offering ideas to the upper levels of management, which allows for a feeling of flattening of the organization and access to the leadership that did not exist before.

I think this is a great indication of organizational leadership that allows all levels of employees to have the opportunity to feel involved in the future of the organization. My agency has created a system whereby when an idea is adopted, they credit the originator. When an idea cannot be adopted, there is usually an explanation, which at least shows the originator that the idea was considered.

This flattening of hierarchies, or adoption of hybrid systems, still requires the responsibility for good leadership in the hierarchical structure. To some extent, it can make supervising and leading even more difficult as you approach the point of flattening where no one is in charge. It can be a difficult balancing act.

As I stated, my agency adopted a hybrid approach that I thought worked pretty well. It left the reporting chains but offered some direct access.

Okay, now that we have established that I worked for the Department of Pyramids, another important thing to understand about this agency is that staff frequently rotate job assignments or positions. Assignments are generally called tours of duty, much like the military, though I did not work for the military. Typically, tours are about two to three years long, though there are a few one-year tours because they are specialized or because they are particularly high stress.

This brings me to my career path. This book covers lessons I learned during my first seven tours, totaling 11 of my 26 years in the Department of Pyramids. For the sake of argument and clarity, let's call these tours:

> Entry-level 1 – Two years (initial training and assignment to a major US city)
>
> Entry-level 2 – Two years (initial assignment to an overseas location)
>
> Journeyman 1 – Two years (second assignment to an overseas location)
>
> Journeyman 2 – Two years (First assignment to headquarters)
>
> Mid-level 1 – Two years (Second assignment to headquarters)
>
> Excursion – 1 year (Educational assignment to a master's degree program)
>
> Mid-Level 2 – Three years (Third assignment to an overseas location)
>
> As far as my path through the overall pyramid, it looks something like the diagram in Figure 0.3.

> **Text Box 0.1**
>
> JOURNEYMAN "a person who was trained to do a particular job and who then worked for somebody else" (*Oxford Advanced Learners Dictionary* (2025))

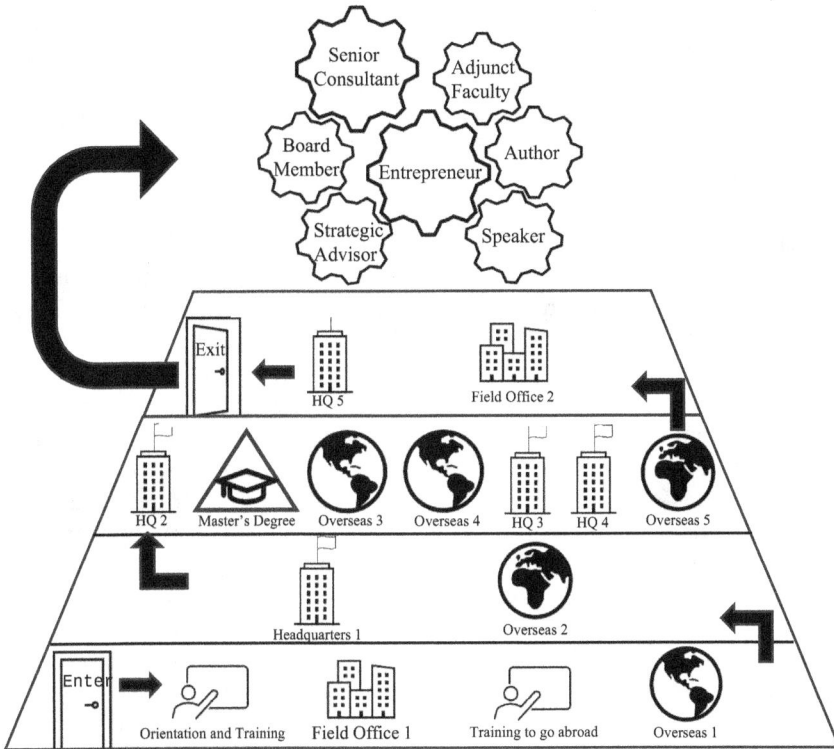

My path through my bureaucracy:
Entry Level – Training, first field office assignment, more training, first overseas assignment
Journeyman Level – Second overseas assignment, first headquarters assignment
Lower Mid-level – Second headquarters assignment, excursion, third and fourth overseas assignments, third and fourth headquarters assignments, fifth overseas assignment
Upper Mid-level – Second field office assignment, final headquarters assignment
After Exiting the Pyramid – Going my own way to build my own company – Entrepreneur, Senior Consultant, Strategic Advisor, Board Member, Author, Speaker, Adjunct Faculty, and more.

Figure 0.3 **A graphical representation of the author's career journey through the bureaucratic pyramid of his agency, with icons to represent each of his assignments at various career stages and the roles the author is fulfilling after his exit from government service.**

My journey through the bureaucratic pyramid gave me the knowledge and skills necessary to embark on my new ventures that are driving me now. You can see that I spent a lot of time (14 years) at the "lower mid-level." Many people faced with this either get discouraged and become just a cog, or look for an early exit. Some, like me, persevere. This perseverance served me well for a couple of reasons. First, I did eventually get promoted into the upper mid-level, and along the way, learned more lessons and built a great network (the value of which I will discuss in Chapter 19). Second, it taught me a lot of lessons about patience and tenacity, which are incredibly important when trying to build your own business. My total journey was 26 years, allowing me to retire and then go on to create my own path.

While the graphic shows my entire career journey, I am focusing this book on the early part of my time in the Pyramid for two reasons. First, this was a foundational period of leadership instruction for me. Second, the target audience for this book is entry- and mid-level personnel who work in bureaucracies, or their own "Department (or company) of Pyramids."

Late in my mid-level 2 assignment, my office underwent a program review. Toward the end, one of the inspectors came into my office and mentioned that in the interviews he had conducted, a lot of people had nice things to say about me and my leadership style. As I was getting ready to leave that position and rotate to another one, several other employees, both in my office and from other offices, expressed that they were sorry to see me go and they hoped that the person following me in the position would be as good and productive as I was. I even found out that our local top management nominated me for a high-level award, which the department approved. All of this got me thinking, maybe there is something I do, some way in which I operate, that helps me be successful, and maybe I can share it with others to help add to their success too. As you will read in Chapter 2, a few of my current values are "explore, collaborate, teach," and this book is a way of sharing or teaching the knowledge I have gained through my exploration of leadership and collaboration and of learning from other leaders. Ultimately, the goal is to help you the reader understand that leadership does not just start at the top; rather, it starts with you.

After all, the goal of any good mid-level bureaucrat is to increase efficiency and productivity.

REFERENCES

Oxford University Press. (n.d.). *Journeyman*. In *Oxford Learner's Dictionaries*. www.oxfordlearnersdictionaries.com/us/definition/english/journeyman

Rockman, B. (2025, March 14). Bureaucracy. In *Britannica*. www.britannica.com/topic/bureaucracy

Part I

Leading yourself

To be a successful leader of others, you need to start by leading yourself. What are your values, what motivates you, what are your goals, what is your routine, and what are your breaking points? I have thought a lot about these matters over the years. Partly, it is because I am reflective by nature, something of an introvert, but also because I have had several opportunities, such as mandatory leadership training, which FORCED me to look at these things.

This is something I recommend: attend some leadership training. Many of my colleagues scoff at the notion and make fun of the instructors, but I have gotten a lot out of the sessions and, as I will discuss more in Part II, "Leading Others," I have used several of the recommendations that they made. If your organization offers leadership training, volunteer to attend. If nothing else, it gives you a break and gets you out of the office for a few days. If you are really lucky, you may gain some insights to make you a better leader.

Insights. This brings us back to the purpose of this part of this book. It is important to reflect on the forces that have individualized us. Think about the influences that shaped you, going back to your childhood. Who were your role models, mentors, and favorite teachers? Why? What did you learn from them and how can that help you now and in the future? These individuals from your youth are often the first leaders you experience and can have a massive impact, both positive and negative, on your own leadership journey.

What are your values and where do they come from? How would you categorize your personality traits and how does that affect your leadership abilities? How hard can you push yourself before you reach your limit, and what do you do to recover? How do you see yourself, and how do others perceive you?

All of these are important questions to answer because they will help you understand your strengths and weaknesses as a leader so that you can better apply those strengths and compensate for the weaknesses.

Here, let me show you: read the chapters and reflect on the lessons at the end of each one. Think through your own story and how it parallels or contrasts with mine. Think about how these experiences, forces, and personalities have prepared you for leadership.

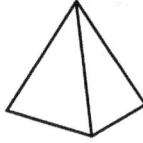

Chapter 1

Understand who shaped you

Differing role models

My parents divorced when I was in the second grade. They both remarried. My dad remarried when I was in the third grade, and my mom remarried when I was in the sixth grade. Both of their second marriages worked for them. I am a little surprised that their marriage to each other lasted as long as it did, because their second marriages are so different from each other.

My mom and stepfather did well in life, and enjoyed the trappings of their success: moderately expensive cars, fur coats, and diamond earrings. They were not millionaires, but they were solidly upper middle class. At one time, one or both sat on boards of directors for charitable foundations, participated in charity auctions, and fit neatly within the upper-middle-class society in which they mingled. But the drama; there was always some sort of drama. It was often like watching a soap opera, especially later, when I was in college or after graduating when I would call, and my mother would work to catch me up on all the gossip she thought I should know about.

My dad and stepmother are very different, still upper middle class, but more reserved. They enjoy the finer things in life, but they don't flaunt it. There is a simple elegance to their lives. They participate in church and occasionally theater, and they spend a couple of weeks a year in Myrtle Beach and another week in Aruba. There is certainly the potential for drama, but they choose not to engage in it. I kind of get the feeling that they had enough drama, so they decided to let it go and avoid it when possible. To an extent, though, it almost seems boring, routine. Some may call that relaxed, but I cannot find myself ready to fully settle into it.

Truthfully, I am probably more like my mother and stepfather, but I feel myself shifting, or at least wanting to shift, more into the mold of my father and stepmother. Ultimately, I would like to take the lessons from each and fuse them. I feel incredibly lucky in my own marriage. Looking at how my parents interact with their second spouses helps me navigate my own marriage and shapes my interactions with others. I try to balance the lessons of all four of my parents.

DOI: 10.1201/9781003650454-3

My mother was caring yet desperately craved attention and affirmation (I am sure this is where I get those same traits, at least the need for attention and affirmation). She was the one who would call if she had not heard from me in three or four days. She wanted to know how I was doing. She celebrated my successes and sympathized with my defeats. She wanted to explore and see the world, going to exotic and far-off places. She was a ball of energy, though her health held her back, which frustrated her.

I remember my mother's reaction to my first car accident, when I was 17 and totaled her car, which I was driving. I expected an outburst, screaming, crying: drama. Instead, I got a calm, collected, "we'll take care of it." Even as we went through the legal process, she worked to make sure that the mitigating factors were presented to the judge, and throughout the episode she stayed like a ship at anchor: solid, steady, rolling with the waves, but always right there in place. Her calmness allayed my fears and reduced my tension.

My stepfather was good with numbers, good at examining contracts and seeing the pitfalls. He was willing to follow my mother around on her adventures. He was good-natured and friendly, a patient teacher. He was not one for drama, which made his relationship with my mother even more interesting. When I was a teenager, he set rules and expected them to be followed, sometimes becoming angry, screaming and yelling when they were not followed. But he was also quick to make amends. I remember once, I was reading a comic book instead of doing my homework (truthfully, a regular occurrence), and he caught me. He grabbed the comic book from me and tore it into pieces. Later that week, though, he quietly put a pair of new comics on my desk. It was sad to watch as he succumbed to Alzheimer's and to see his memory and mind shrivel before he passed.

My father is a planner. He always has a project of some sort, always working toward a goal. In his sixties, he decided he wanted to try his hand at being a television commentator. So, he started his own show on a local cable network. When he was growing up, he lived in several countries, and hearing his stories fostered my desire to get out and see the world. My father is continuously learning. He is one of those people who is always acquiring new skills and ideas, because they never know when these might come in handy. That is probably one of the biggest traits I got from him. I also got the knack for planning out a project and then following the plan to complete the project.

My stepmother is good at seeing the bigger picture. She keeps things on track and makes sure that as my father delves deeply into some topic or another, he comes up for air often enough to stay on the overall course. When one of my siblings has a real problem, she is the one who steps up and says, "Okay, here is how we start to fix it." She is factual (though with a penchant for hyperbole), solid, no drama, this is the big picture and where we need to go from here. Whenever I had to make a major life decision (which college will be best, should I change my major, should I take this job), I always reached out to my father and stepmother and bounced my ideas off them.

Parents are not the only influence, though they are big ones. There are three other major influences that help shape our character and mold us into the adults we become: friends, teachers, and mentors.

I was not one of the popular "in-crowd" people in high school. I had a handful of friends, though, and they really helped balance me, two of them in particular. I am still friends with them to this day.

Mike is a fun-loving, happy, well-adjusted, down-to-earth guy. He went to the major Jesuit high school in town, followed by a Jesuit university. He is married to a wonderful woman and has two great kids. In high school, Mike and I would hang out on the side porch of my house and debate the flavor and texture qualities of various brands of root beer (yes, you read that right, root beer) to try to determine which was the best. Mike is a music connoisseur and introduced me to some of my favorite groups. Mike and I took a road trip together to look at colleges during our senior year of high school, and I think that permanently cemented our friendship. When my first engagement broke up, Mike and I spent a fun week at Disney World in Orlando, since that was supposed to be my honeymoon and it was already paid for.

Mike once said that he lives vicariously through me as I bounced around the globe and constantly changed assignments within the Department of Pyramids. This is funny to me, because there are times when I envy the stability he has and the closeness he shares with his extended family. He also has a lot of determination. He went to night school to get his MBA, completing it just as the market crashed and the unemployment rate skyrocketed. Still, he keeps his priorities in order and walks an even path, always moving forward.

Josh is a long-haired, vegetarian, Buddhist who loves baseball and has never enjoyed music. He is incredibly smart; in fact, he skipped kindergarten because he had taught himself to read. Hanging out with Josh introduced me to a lot of different concepts and realities, particularly for a seventh grader: he and his dad were the only Buddhists I knew. He introduced me to *Dungeons & Dragons*, comic books, and science fiction books; we played a lot of soccer and baseball in the front yard; and he had a love for learning and knowledge that was contagious. Now, he teaches calculus and advanced mathematics in a public high school and holds two master's degrees. Josh has an appreciation for the world around him and a fabulous easygoing manner. He received his second master's degree when his first son was born, and he took a year's sabbatical from teaching to have a more flexible schedule to focus time on his family during his son's first year of life.

What either of these guys saw in me that caused them to put up with me is a mystery. Sure, we had some shared interests, but the three of us came from different family styles and very different approaches to life. It was those differences and broadening experiences that helped shape and mold my own character, and that continues to this day.

Teachers are often referred to as role models. I had several who influenced my life and thinking. I was involved in a high school chorus with a fantastic teacher who touched the lives of many of his students. When he passed away, the outpouring of emotion was substantial. The lessons I learned from him were not just about music, but also about life, responsibility, and integrity.

Every year the chorus would go on "tour" to a different city during spring break. Think about this for a minute: between 100 and 120 tenth through twelfth graders on three tour buses for a week in a different city each year. Sure, my teacher had some additional parents along as chaperones, but the simple fact that he was able to lead these trips year after year for more than 20 years shows both that he had incredible faith in his students, and that they (we) had incredible respect for him. In order to accomplish this feat every year, my teacher had come up with rules and a code of conduct that each of us was required to sign. Many of these rules were simply to protect us (curfews, mandatory buddy system, no student contact with the hotel staff, etc.), and others were designed to help us present a positive image (dress code, rules of behavior, etc.).

You were expected to follow the rules. While I do not remember anyone in my three years with the chorus actually being sent home, there were a couple of close calls. Typically, though, when there was an infraction of the rules, my teacher would pull the offender aside and have a frank, pointed discussion on what had happened and why it had happened. These discussions were NOT one-sided; he wanted the other side of the story and then would determine if the infraction warranted additional sanctions (sitting out a performance, being restricted to the hotel, being sent home, etc.). I know this because I had one of these discussions with him in my senior year, when I ran afoul of the rules. But the conversation showed the kind of man and leader he was. Yes, I came out of the conversation ashamed of my behavior, but also with a sense of his integrity and a desire to live up to his standards. He did not just beat you down and chastise you for what you had done: he showed you the path to bettering yourself.

Two other teachers who shaped my thinking were a sociology professor in my undergraduate program and an ethics professor in my master's degree program. The sociology professor introduced me to the study of demographics and a view of events from a larger, societal perspective. My ethics professor urged me, and the rest of the class, to challenge our thinking about the status quo and acceptable behavior in bureaucracies.

Understanding these influences and what you learned from them is a great starting point on the path to leading yourself. The process of reflecting and being able to articulate these influences for yourself and to others increases your leadership capabilities. It also increases trust in yourself and can help you overcome impostor syndrome.

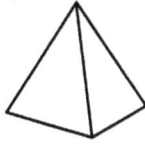

Here is the lesson:
Know what shaped you. If you cannot coherently explain the forces in your life that shaped and developed your personality and leadership style, how are you going to gain credibility to lead others? Think about these forces and influences, and be able to talk about them and explain them. The ability to articulate these influences will help you understand them better and the effects they have had on you, positive and negative.

Chapter 2

Define your leadership values

Lessons from Scouting and beyond

A Scout is: Trustworthy, Loyal, Helpful, Friendly, Courteous, Kind, Obedient, Cheerful, Thrifty, Brave, Clean, and Reverent (Boy Scouts of America, 1990).

I admit it, I'm a Boy Scout. In fact, I'm an Eagle Scout, and I'm proud of the accomplishment. I learned a lot from Scouts. I don't think I really appreciated and understood how much I learned until I was in my late twenties. For those who don't know them, or don't remember them, the words at the opening of this chapter are the Scout Laws. Each one is a principle to try to live by. Scouting, both Boy Scouts (now Scouting America) and Girl Scouts, is, at its core, a leadership development program. Look back at the words and reflect on how each one by itself is a noble aspiration, and how together they are the embodiment of civility, honor, and respect.

Your values may well have a different source, but through this chapter I'll explore these as an example that will hopefully cause you to reflect on and articulate your own.

I was not the best Scout. I did what I was supposed to, slightly more than the minimum to get by. As I mentioned, I earned my Eagle Scout award, and I suppose that makes me much better than the statistically average Scout. I earned all 21 merit badges, and even a few extra. I served in leadership positions, and I completed my Eagle Scout Leadership Service Project. I was 17 when I finally completed all the requirements. The maximum age before which the requirements must be completed is 18. Technically, based on the time intervals required for the upper ranks, the youngest you can be when you attain Eagle Scout is 13. I know a couple of Scouts who accomplished that feat, attaining Eagle Scout before they turned 14. They were impressive and motivated. Me … yeah, not so much.

But I did finish. Then, when I was in college, I started to give back, going with the troop for summer camp to ensure there would be enough adult leaders. After a couple of summers, I had other things to do and fell out of it for a couple of years, but during my first overseas assignment, there was a Scout troop affiliated with the US Embassy. Understanding how hard it can

DOI: 10.1201/9781003650454-4

be to get adult volunteers and, as an Eagle Scout, wanting to be a role model for the younger scouts, I volunteered again to help.

It was during this time that I really started to figure out how much Scouting had shaped me and how the values of Scouting are ingrained in me. I started to compare the values of Scouting to the ethics training I received as part of my job. I started to really think about and reflect on the values enumerated in the Scout Laws.

Trustworthy: literally, worthy of trust and confidence. Someone who will do the right, honorable, and moral thing. A trustworthy person can be told things in confidence and be expected to keep that confidence. A trustworthy person does not steal, connive, or intentionally breach trust and confidence. For me, trustworthiness has a lot to do with honor and respect. To be honorable, you must show respect for those who have bestowed their trust upon you. Trustworthiness, honor, and respect are all things that are built up slowly over time, but are very delicate and can be dashed in an instance of carelessness and disregard.

Loyal. Someone who stays faithful to his friends, colleagues, and obligations. Someone who will stick with you, even when it is difficult, even when others abandon you. A loyal person will tell you the truth, even when it is hard to hear. Having loyal friends is incredibly important, especially during hard times. Being a loyal friend is just as important. Loyalty is not always easy; it is not always quick; and it may not meet with immediate gratification or reward. The society we live in does not promote loyalty (reality television, advertisers trying to get you to switch brands, political pundits striving for divisiveness, etc.), but loyalty is a critically important component of leadership.

Helpful. A helpful person will go out of their way to ensure you get what you need. They will lend assistance and answer questions. They will drop what they are working on without expressing annoyance, just to help someone out. I am a generally helpful person, almost to a fault. I am often in the middle of ten different projects because I offer to assist others and will drop what I am doing to help someone else. As a leader, if you see someone struggling with a project or a task, you are responsible to the overall mission to help set them on the right path. Not only does this lead to the accomplishment of the particular task, but it sets an example for others to follow. Taking the task from them and doing it yourself is not the goal. The idea is to help them accomplish the task, giving them guidance, advice, and assistance so they can carry it out themselves.

Friendly. Smile, say hello, have a positive attitude, and try to help others. You never know what insight you will gain into people and situations by simply being friendly. This is not the fake, plastic smile or the overly zealous, smother them with kindness kind of friendly. The goal here is a genuine caring for others, with a welcoming smile, a firm handshake, and a "how can I help you" attitude. Bureaucracies are NOT known for being friendly.

They are known for "take a number, what's your problem, fill out this form, check back in 30 days. NEXT." That is the unfortunate stereotype, but the reality is, I have run into some fantastically friendly people while trying to accomplish various tasks such as getting a new Social Security card, renewing my driver's license, and obtaining a bank loan. Also, you never know how being friendly yourself may impact others. I was once in line at the gate to ask a question before I boarded an airplane. The airline employee was having a difficult time with the man in front of me, and she looked exasperated when he finally finished his turn. I simply walked up to the counter, gave the employee a smile and a small shrug, and said jokingly, "Any chance I can get an upgrade because it's Monday and you're having a great day?" She burst out laughing and gave me the upgrade. Friendly.

Courteous. A courteous person thinks of others before thinking of themselves. Little civilities such as holding doors, helping with packages, offering seats to those who need them. It seems sometimes that we as a society have lost our basic courtesy. There was a man at one of my workplaces who is the embodiment of courtesy. He is a big, tough-looking guy, Army Special Forces, but he is the politest, most courteous person I know or have ever known. He defines the term "gentleman." Watching him and how he interacted with people made me want to try harder to be more like him.

Kind. The Boy Scout Slogan is "do a good turn daily." The goal of "kind" is to focus on the needs of others. Maybe this is volunteering some time reading to the blind, serving in a shelter for the homeless, or participating in some other charitable endeavor. Better, though, are the simple, day-in-day-out events where we could all share a little kindness: offering to help carry a package, giving up a taxi to someone who needs it more, letting the person in front of you into your lane while driving, letting someone with just a few items check out before us in the grocery store. We have unfortunately become a society where "me, myself, and I" often become the priorities over "you," as in "me first," or "I'll serve myself, then you," and "I have somewhere to be, so you can wait."

A couple of years ago, as the world was in the throes of the COVID-19 pandemic, I became a member of an online movement called the Kindness Games. The founders, Tim Wenzel and Lee Oughton, recognized that in the rapid shift to work from home, a lot of people were suffering from lack of contact and interaction, feeling forgotten. Tim and Lee started a game to record video tributes to people who had shown them kindness in their professional journeys. These were people who had mentored them, inspired them, given them opportunities, or just been kind to them. The goal was to return that kindness in two ways, letting the tribute recipient know the kindness was still appreciated, and highlighting to the rest of the world the awesomeness of the tribute recipient. I had run across Tim through a leadership organization we both participated in called Whole and Intentional Leader Development (WiLD Leaders), and I was following him on LinkedIn when he and Lee started the Kindness Games. Eventually, I could not resist the calling to participate myself and I have posted more than 60 tribute videos. The story of my overall journey through the Kindness Games and that of many of the other original participants can be found in our book, *The Kindness Games: How a Single Post Changed Our Mindset about Community* (2023). I am still involved with the Kindness Games to this day, and it is amazing how the movement has evolved and the friendships I have gained through it, all because a couple of guys decided the world needed a little bit more kindness.

Obedient. An obedient person follows the rules; they are law-abiding, and they follow instructions. I am not suggesting blind obedience or fealty, but there is a general sense that if you tell an obedient person to do something, they will do it. As I said, they follow the rules and are law-abiding, show up for work on time, are not disruptive in the workplace, and follow the rules.

Cheerful. Do you have a positive or negative outlook on life? Do you see difficulties, or challenges to overcome? Some people see cheerful, and they think "bubbly and annoying." That is not what I mean by cheerful. I mean seeing opportunity in adversity, looking on the bright side, seeing the glass as half-full. I had a supervisor once who marveled at my ability to take a blow, absorb it, deal with it, and then say, "okay, next." I do not do everything right, and I have screwed up some of my tasks substantially, but my attitude has always been one in which I learn from the mistakes, move on, and try to not repeat them. Rather than let a situation get me down, I try to stay upbeat and positive.

Another way of looking at the value "cheerful" is to call it welcoming. When someone new starts with your team, how do you greet them? Are you welcoming and show that you are happy to have them, or do you have a chip on your shoulder that says, "you are nothing until you prove yourself to me"? Which one of these do you think inspires more confidence and productivity?

Thrifty. Are you careful with money? Thrifty does not mean cheap. It does not mean you always go with the lowest bidder. It means you balance the cost and effect. A truly thrifty person will look for good deals on high-quality products that will have a decent lifespan and only buy what they actually need and will use. Thrifty is a good value to have when you are in a position to manage other people's money, such as that of your company or a nonprofit organization. As you rise in management positions, you will likely become responsible for managing budgets and accounts. Having a thrifty mindset helps you understand the cost-versus-value proposition. As a leader, being able to articulate that proposition will be incredibly important. For example, I was elected president of the local employee association at two of my overseas assignments. I needed to be a good steward for the funds we contributed and raised. I used my thrifty mindset as we embarked on projects to ensure we were getting the best value for the organization. I also had to convince the board and membership that the investments were worth it, sharing this value of thriftiness to engender trust and influence, which are foundational to leadership.

Brave. A brave person is willing to take risks, to stand up in the face of adversity. There is a significant difference between "brave" and "foolhardy," though sometimes finding the line between them can be difficult, especially when you are too close to a situation or have too much invested in a topic. It takes a lot of courage to look at the status quo and challenge it, especially from an inferior position. It can be difficult to manage up and tell your supervisor that he or she is wrong and that something needs to be done differently. Sometimes the issue will not be worth "falling on your sword" over. Other times, the issue may be of such importance that if you do not get the response you believe is needed, you will have to marshal your arguments and go one level or more higher until you reach a level at which you can get your point across. You also need to remember that just because you win, does not mean there won't be consequences, especially if you had to go over someone's head to get the result you were aiming for.

Clean. A clean person is not just physically clean, making sure to take a shower and brush their teeth every day. A clean person is also "morally straight" as phrased in the Boy Scout Oath. A clean person is fair and does not cheat. A clean person does not engage in gossip or double-dealing, promising something to someone with no intention of following through, or intentionally setting traps for people to fall into, just so he or she can get ahead. A lot of bureaucracies encourage a system of stepping on those below you to get ahead, but real leadership is bringing the people below you up with you.

Reverent. There has been a lot of debate about the place of religion in the development of values. As it was explained to me when I was a young Scout, who was questioning if not the existence of God, then at least the correctness of organized religion: you must understand that there is a power higher and mightier than yourself. You need to have respect for that power and for others who believe differently. You do not need to be a Christian to be a Scout: Scouting America currently has agreements in place with 38 different religious organizations for the achievement of religious emblems that may be worn as part of the Scout uniform. These include several denominations of Christianity as well as Islam, Judaism, Hinduism, Buddhism, Baha'i, and Zoroastrianism, to name a few.

The Scout Laws are values that have been ingrained in me. I am frequently looking for ways to better live up to these values. I have other values as well. A couple of years ago, I was reflecting on three words that reflect my values, and I came up with: explore, collaborate, teach. Explore—find new areas of interest and dig into them. Collaborate—find communities of purpose in those areas and work to learn and share with them. Teach—share with others what I have learned. While I was scaling my pyramid, I found that these values served me well as I rotated positions frequently, got involved in projects, and helped to develop the next generation of leaders around me. I model these values now through my work as an entrepreneur, as an adjunct faculty member at a university, and in other projects I involve myself in.

Finally, I joined the international service organization Rotary International last year. I like their four-way test of truth, fairness, mutual benefit, and building goodwill and better friendships (Rotary International, n.d.). I try to reflect on those values in my interactions as well.

Your values may well be very different. My goal in detailing my values through the Scout Laws and the other points above is to show an articulation of them and examples. As you develop your leadership style, the first person you need to be able to lead is yourself, which is why Part 1 of this book has this focus. Part of leading yourself is understanding your values and living them faithfully with integrity.

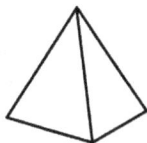

Here is the lesson:
Know what your values are. If you can identify your values and live
by them yourself, you can be a role model for others. If you con-
sistently live by your values and show integrity, people will be more
likely to follow you.

REFERENCES

Boy Scouts of America. (1990). *Boy Scout Handbook* (10th ed.). Boy Scouts of America.

Rotary International. (n.d.). The Four-Way Test. www.rotary.org/en/about-rotary/four-way-test

Chapter 3

Understanding your strengths and weaknesses

Technology, people, vision, and energy

I admit I often like technology more than I like people. Computers are logical, emotionless, and generally do what you tell them to. If they don't do what you tell them, you are probably doing it wrong, or if there is a problem with the machine, you can easily replace it. With people, this process can be much harder.

A little insight into me: I was nominated for my department's annual agency-wide technology innovation award three times and won it once, even though I am not in the IT field. I am good at envisioning and executing system/process integration and designing relatively simple solutions using existing technology to solve complex problems. I enjoy this a lot. It is like a challenge or a puzzle. If I encounter a glitch in something I am working on, I will go through it in the minutest detail to find what I did wrong, what I missed, and fix it. I can be obsessive in these areas.

Where I sometimes fall short, though, and where I am constantly trying to improve, is in engaging with people. Recognizing this weakness is part of leadership. No matter how wonderful my idea of the moment might be, I know that I need to be able to bring other people into it so I can lead them and, eventually, lead the organization.

I am bad at remembering people's names and where I know them from. I am horrendous at remembering birthdays. On the Myers-Briggs Type Inventory, I skew INTJ: Introverted, Intuitive, Thinking, and Judging. This combination is sometimes referred to as the "Strategic Mastermind" personality type because the combination of attributes is strong for visionary leadership, planning, and logical connections (The Myers-Briggs Company, 2025).

Many people confuse introversion as shyness, but really it is about energy. I get a lot of energy by working on a problem or project on my own. There is a great book that goes into more detail about this called *The Introvert Advantage*, by Marti Olsen Laney. At the beginning of chapter 1, Laney explains, "The strongest distinguishing characteristic of introverts is their

DOI: 10.1201/9781003650454-5

energy source: Introverts draw energy from their internal world of ideas, emotions and impressions" (Laney, 2002, p. 19).

The opposite of introversion is extroversion. Substitute the "E" for "I" on the Myers-Briggs scale and you get ENTJ. This personality type is often referred to as the "Field Marshal" for their ability to see the big picture of a strategy (even though they often do not concern themselves with the concrete details) and rally people around it. They draw energy from interacting with others and thrive in social settings. As extroverts, they flourish in the social world (The Myers-Briggs Company, 2025).

It takes effort for me to interact at social functions, and I find it tiring, even exhausting. I often overcompensate and feel as if I am coming off as disingenuous, which adds to my discomfort.

Importantly, I recognize this as a weakness, and I have found strategies for dealing with it. I sometimes slip out of social events or at least find a quiet corner to get away from all of the mental and emotional noise. I am still not great at small talk. I am getting better at large gatherings, though, mostly because a friend of mine once gave me an invaluable piece of advice: "find the small group within the large group." Instead of trying to make order out of the chaos of the overall event, I float around until I find a small group that I can connect with. If I have a day of back-to-back meetings, I will take a break partway through to engage in a mindfulness meditation or just a breathing exercise to settle myself or recharge.

There are a lot of strengths that come from being an INTJ, especially when it comes to the "strategic mastermind" side of problem-solving: being logical, analytical, and innovative.

For example, I once had a supervisor who would list out the tasks for the office as a written list. You may think, okay a list: that is good, everyone knows what they are supposed to do, great. I was frustrated by it, though. To me, the organization and flow were confusing. The tasks were listed multiple times, and it was not clear who was actually responsible and who was the backup. So, my response was to turn the list around and make it into a chart: tasks down one side, names at the top, check marks at the intersections. Much better, clearer, no more confusion; even my supervisor saw the value in the new layout.

Another time there was a question about a business process for visitors to access our facility. The question was, why were people getting stuck at a certain point in the process and either failing to register their visitors or, alternatively, overwhelming the system with unnecessary requests? Why was there confusion? My response: a flowchart. I created a flowchart, listing out the process, decisions points, and all the variables.

We found that people were being confused not because of the process, but because of the vocabulary used to differentiate between "visitors" and "temporary duty employees." Many offices referred to temporary duty employees (people sent from headquarters to work in the office for any-where from a day to a year) as "visitors." My office considered "visitors" to be nonemployees coming for a meeting or event. We needed to understand why these other offices kept entering visitor access requests into the mix for temporary duty employees. Once we had the flowchart and checked it with those other offices, it was like a light bulb went on. They realized they were taking steps they did not need to, bogging down the entry system, and adding to the confusion. We realized how to guide them better to streamline the process. Win-win.

I did this a lot when I first arrived at a new tour of duty. I would look at the processes that were in place and decide whether they needed to be changed or not, at a glance, with a snap judgment, even if the procedure had been in place for years. My personality type automatically looks at things and says, "okay, how can we make this better, more efficient, run more smoothly, be more productive?" I personally tend to try to apply techno-logical solutions to these problems.

At the end of our year together, my supervisor simply looked at me, saw the improvements I had made, and just said, "Man, you really see things differently than most people, don't you?" Yep, I sure do. The funny thing is that even after we no longer worked in the same office, this former super-visor called me or emailed me every couple of weeks to look at something he was working on, or even something he was about to start working on, to get my take on it.

Now, please understand that being INTJ is not a perfect bed of roses. Just like any other personality type, it comes with baggage. I mentioned the issues with social interactions earlier, but there are other areas that I need to pay attention to as well.

For example, as I am processing information and ideas, I often make leaps of logic, which, even when I can explain them, still baffle many people. When someone comes to me with a problem, I try instantly to find a solu-tion, but sometimes what people are looking for is simply a sounding board so they can come up with their own solutions. I sometimes come to snap judgments when I haven't even heard all the arguments.

Another area in which I have learned I need to be careful is having respect for seniority and authority. For whatever reason, I usually cannot accept and respect that simply because someone has a hefty title or rank, they must be right. I tend to challenge authority when I think the authority is wrong, or as in the case of the examples above, I just go do what I think is the better choice without consulting the authority. This has gotten me into some trouble, especially with supervisors who firmly believe in the chain of command. Sometimes, my attitude may even seem to border on personal disrespect, though I often do not even realize it. At other times, my contempt for the "people in charge," and their lack of logic, can be so thick I can almost taste it. This is particularly true when I believe they are relying on an outmoded status quo rather than trying to move things forward.

While I had taken the Myers-Briggs inventory a couple of times before in college or other seminars, it was not until the agency's leadership training that I really learned how I could use the information. I got a lot out of the leadership training provided by my department. I think there are few who will admit this. Many managers believe they already know it all; otherwise, they never would have been promoted into management positions. One of the biggest takeaways I got out of the training was not about managing others as much as it was about managing myself: adjusting my management style to suit the needs of others.

One issue the leadership training helped me realize is that I DO see things differently than a lot of people. Sometimes, when I give a task to a subordinate, I have a very clear picture in my head of the result that I want, and I forget that the subordinate cannot see that picture, so the instructions I give are not as clear as they could be. Occasionally, this freedom for the employee results in a product that is even better than I envisioned, but often, I simply end up redoing parts to make it turn out the way that I wanted.

The key here is that I know this *now*. Going through my first leadership training course really opened a lot for me because I finally got it: how I see things and interpret things is often different from others. As a leader, I need to be aware of this so I can fine-tune my leadership style to suit the needs of the people I am leading.

Now, if I see someone struggling with implementing my vision, instead of simply taking the task away from them and doing it myself, I have been taught strategies for instructing them in different ways to guide them better. The difference is huge—take the project away and make them feel like a failure or find a way to help them succeed. As a leader, you want your employees to have that feeling of success and have them understand that you helped them get there. On a larger scale, once you get to know your employees' strengths and weaknesses, and their approach to tasks, you can better divide up those tasks with greater efficiency.

Understanding your strengths and weaknesses is a constant process. However, the work is worth it. As I mentioned at the beginning of this chapter, INTJs are sometimes referred to as the "Strategic Masterminds." According to the Myers-Briggs Company, though it is estimated that only 2%–3% of the population falls into this category, "INTJ people are often able to define a compelling, long-range vision, and can devise innovative solutions to complex problems" (The Myers-Briggs Company, 2025).

These attributes and the work that I had done to hone my strengths and find ways to compensate for my weaknesses really came through when I was working on another project that transformed how my department approached emergency management. My reviewing officer (my boss's boss) wrote of me in my employee evaluation:

For those familiar with the glacial pace at which bureaucracies change, one can easily understand the inherent frustrations and roadblocks to be expected when a product in use for in excess of 30 years is suddenly told to transform! To Chris' credit, he not only totally embraced the assignment, he did so in a manner that both assuaged the feelings of all involved and set forth an operational plan to ensure success. What has developed as a result of Chris' tremendous effort is the exact web-based system initially envisioned and the gratitude of embassies that were able to shred their archaic and antiquated ways of doing business. Hyperbole? Perhaps a tad, but please understand that this is perhaps the best example of transformational engineering the Department has enjoyed to date.

Sometimes, you can capture lightning in a bottle: the once-in-a-career opportunity to really make a difference in your organization. But as is often said, luck favors the prepared.

Understanding your strengths and weaknesses is important preparation. If you understand them, then you can look for projects that play to your strengths.

At the same time, being aware of your weaknesses and having the ability to find strategies to overcome them will help too. This may be strategies you yourself can employ, or it may be an understanding that you need someone else with a complementary strength to balance out your weakness.

The best leaders do not necessarily have all the answers and nor think they can do it all. The best leaders attract and surround themselves with people who know more than they themselves do about key topics, and with people who are stronger in the leaders' areas of weakness. But you can only do this if you know and understand your own strengths and weaknesses.

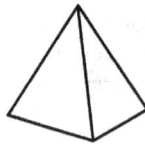

Here is the lesson:
Know your strengths and weaknesses as a leader. Try to find ways to balance these and learn ways to improve in areas where you are weak, without compromising in areas where you are strong. Try to get honest, active feedback to help you improve.

REFERENCES

Laney, M. O. (2002). *The Introvert Advantage: How Quiet People Can Thrive in an Extrovert World* (New York, Workman), 19.

The Myers-Briggs Company. (2025). *INTJ: MBTI personality profile.* https://eu.themyersbriggs.com/en/tools/MBTI/MBTI-personality-Types/INTJ

Chapter 4

Understanding limits
It's not a stroke, just a migraine

Like I said in the last chapter, I can become a little obsessive when it comes to problem-solving. I am also very logical in my orientation. This helps make me a good troubleshooter. While you can train people to fix problems that are identified, it is much harder to train them in how to identify a problem in the first place. Therefore, I often take on the troubleshooting part myself, which once led me to a major lesson on leadership that has stayed with me, but that I still need to remind myself of from time to time. The lesson is about learning where your breaking points are, recognizing when you are approaching them, and making a change to ensure you are taking care of yourself.

The story goes like this: During my second overseas assignment (Journeyman 1), I oversaw a major project involving capital construction and installation of hydraulic equipment. A contractor completed the work, but because the nature of the project fell under my program's purview, I was the on-site representative to oversee the contractor and ensure that our site stayed secure throughout the construction process. I was supported by a cadre of technical experts from my agency's headquarters who came out several times throughout the project to inspect it and to certify it as complete. Then, the experts left, followed shortly by the contractors.

I had heard from other locations about similar projects that experienced problems within months of the contractors leaving, so I had a sense that we would have issues as well.

Three days.

Yes, no kidding. Three days after the contractors left, stuff started to break. Now, the contractors had trained the mechanics from the facilities maintenance office how to fix things, but they had not taught them how to troubleshoot the systems. In this, I was uniquely qualified: the systems fell under my area of responsibility, and I am a born troubleshooter. Therefore, every time the system failed, the first thing the mechanics did was, instead of checking the system themselves, they called me.

DOI: 10.1201/9781003650454-6

At first, I was excited by this. I was a journeyman-level bureaucrat, hoping for advancement, and here was a chance to show off my skills, solve a problem, learn something new, and share the solution with others. The problem was that after a couple of weeks, I started to become frustrated. Why couldn't they troubleshoot or fix it themselves? Why does the damn thing keep breaking? Why doesn't headquarters require the contractors to come back to fix it once and for all?

Eventually, the phone would ring, I would see the mechanic's number in the caller ID, and I would just feel exhausted, physically and emotionally exhausted. I had reached my breaking point, but I did not realize it. I did not realize the damage I was doing to myself, nor the truly frightening experience I was about to put myself through.

For a couple of days, I had noticed that when I was in certain offices, particularly those that were windowless and lit completely by fluorescent lights, the light looked like it was underwater, and when I looked at the light directly, it had a hazy rainbow effect. I also recognized the feeling of exhaustion I was experiencing every time I took a call from the mechanics. On an unrelated issue, I had been experiencing some back pain (side note: always make sure you have a good chair and a good mattress), so I had gone to the doctor and was given a pain reliever. While I cannot trace medication to my initial episode, I am sure it was a contributing factor.

So, on a Monday in December, I was sitting at my desk, working on whatever report I was trying to complete, when the phone rang. I looked at the caller ID: the mechanics, again. I answered the phone: okay, the hydraulic system is acting up again. Okay, fine, I will come to take a look and show you, again, what to check to find out what is wrong so you can fix it. I will be there in a few minutes/ I need to finish this section of the report.

I sat back in my chair, exhausted. I noticed a feeling of tingling in my right hand. Thinking it was merely "asleep" because I had been leaning on my wrist while typing, I tried to shake it to "wake it up." The feeling of tingling did not go away; instead, it started to advance up my arm. Now I was a little concerned. Was this a side effect of the medication I was taking for my back? I decided to go to the health unit.

Unfortunately, the physician's assistant was out at an appointment, but by the time I walked across the campus of my worksite, the feeling had gone away, so I just wrote it off and decided to ignore it. I went back to my office, sat back down, and looked at the report I was working on. Then I remembered the phone call from the mechanic, and, within seconds, it hit me.

The feeling of tingling started in my right hand again, but this time, it spread fast. It raced up my right arm and over the right side of my body. I started to get scared. The feeling spread down my right leg and up the right side of my face and head. I needed help, fast. I decided to try to call my wife.

I reached for the phone but came up with the computer mouse. "No, that's not right," I thought. I put the mouse down and reached for the phone again. Again, I came up with the computer mouse. Finally, on my third attempt, I got the phone in my hand.

Now I had another problem: I could not remember my home phone number. I called out to my secretary in the next room and asked her what my number was. She laughed a little and told me. I got through the first two or three digits and then could not remember the rest of what she had told me, so I asked her again. She got up from her desk and poked her head in my office, repeating the number. Again, I only got through the first two digits.

At that point, she took the phone from my hand, put it back in the cradle, and told me she would call my wife. She then called her husband, who worked in an office down the hall, and had him walk me to the health unit. I could barely walk because of the numbness and tingling on the right side of my body, and I was continuing to lose muscle control. Somehow, we made it to the health unit anyway.

Luckily, when we got to the health unit, the physician's assistant had returned from her appointment. She quickly got me onto a gurney and did a quick examination. I was exhibiting all the symptoms of a major stroke. I was 29 years old. I had been married for just over a year. I had my whole life ahead of me. I was terrified.

My wife arrived. I tried to explain to her what I was feeling and experiencing, but the words came out slurred and/or I said words I did not intend: left instead of right, leg instead of arm. My wife was actually a little amused by this. I started to cry. My wife stayed by me and told me everything would be all right, but I could tell she was now scared too. The physician's assistant came back and inserted an IV to keep me hydrated and to add medication if needed.

As the fluid entered my bloodstream, the most amazing sensation spread over my body. It felt like all the numbness and tingling was pushed along out of the way by the fluid, but then it felt like it all built up like an overflowing dam of pressure in my head. and my eyes felt like they wanted to burst from their sockets. On the upside, I could speak clearly again and had control over my limbs. On the downside, I had a splitting headache. I was sent home and told to rest with ice packs on my head to help with the headache. The headache lasted for three days.

At home, I made myself a little nest of blankets and pillows in the living room (I was too weak to climb the stairs). I turned on the ceiling fan and closed all the curtains to block out the light. After a day and a half, I was finally able to sit up enough to watch television. I went for a CAT scan, which was inconclusive. Finally, by Thursday, I was feeling well enough to get myself up off the floor and start to think about cleaning up my little nest. I was still experiencing intermittent headaches, usually when I moved too quickly.

As I bent down to pick up a blanket, I started to think about everything waiting for me at work. Then it started again, this time in my left thigh.

As it happened, a friend was over at our house and her father is a neurologist. When the numbness and tingling started in my left calf, she got him on the phone and was able to describe the very visible progression of this attack as it raced up my left leg, up my torso, down my arm, and finally up my head and face. The doctor on the phone, hearing the description of what was going on and the explanation of the previous event, opined that I might actually be experiencing a migraine. He had me lie down on the floor, turn the ceiling fan back on, turn off the lights, and breathe deeply and slowly. The symptoms started to recede. The next call was to the health unit, to let them know what was going on.

Because I had had two episodes in under a week, the decision was made to medically evacuate me on the next available commercial flight to the nearest regional medical center. Since we were not sure if I would have another episode or when, my wife was sent with me as a nonmedical escort. We had a great two weeks in London.

It turns out that the break was just what I needed. Except for the cold that I caught on the flight over to London, I did not experience any problems while we were there. I have not had a full-blown migraine since.

I had a series of tests while in London to rule out a stroke as a possible cause. I also had a good talk with the neurologist about what had happened, and he provided me with some great information about likely causes and triggers. Since then, I have never had another full episode. It appears that my primary trigger is frustration. I had found my breaking point.

While I have not had another full-blown migraine, I have experienced the early onset symptoms, the swimming vision and feeling of exhaustion. What is different is that I now know what this means and see it as a big, bold, flashing, neon sign that I need to make a change. I need either to walk away from what I am working on for a while, or maybe even to give the project over to someone else completely. Sometimes I can just engage in the deep breathing exercises or take a walk for ten or twenty minutes and that is enough to reset myself. Other times, I need to lie down and sleep, sometimes for an hour, occasionally for 12–14 hours, depending on how far along I have allowed my symptoms to get.

I share this story because self-care is crucially important to leadership, especially leading yourself. This experience taught me very important lessons about that, and a growing body of research supports this point.

For example, in an article for *Forbes*, Heather McArthur concluded, "Incorporating self-care as a fundamental leadership competency is essential for creating resilient leaders who inspire and engage their teams" (McArthur, 2024). Throughout her article she draws on research on the links between self-care, resilience, and prevention of burnout. She also concludes with this,

By setting an example through intentional self-care practices, leaders can pave the way for a healthier, more productive workplace culture. Embracing self-care is not just a personal benefit but a strategic leadership choice that can redefine the success of organizations in today's challenging environment.

This perspective is backed up by a study conducted by the National Institute of Health in 2022, which found that "leader self-care in terms of personal efforts to manage one's health at work may play an important role in two ways: by improving their leadership behavior or through a direct role-modeling effect on employee self-care" (Klug et al, 2022, p. 1). The results of the study provide "initial evidence why leader self-care matters: leader self-care tends to go along with staff care, which in turn relates to employee health" (Klug et al, 2022, p. 12).

Palena Neale, in an article published in *Harvard Business Review*, provided "A Self-Care Checklist for Leaders" (Neale, 2024). In the article, she reviews some of the reasons why leaders fail to incorporate appropriate self-care into their regular routines, such as organizational and cultural norms, time, and even lack of knowledge on how to properly practice self-care. Neale then provides a series of strategies to "set yourself up for success", followed by a five-point checklist for caring for the body, mind, relationships, capacity for choice, and growth. She states she has used this with hundreds of leaders and recommends taking 15 minutes a week to reflect on your health in each of these areas.

Understanding and practicing self-care is important for leading yourself and leading others. This includes physical, mental, and emotional self-care. There is a saying that goes "the brightest shooting star burns out the fastest." Burnout is real. If you feel it is starting to happen, it is time to turn down the heat.

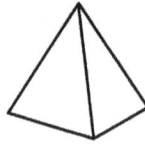

Here is the lesson:
Know your stressors, breaking points, and recovery strategies. If you cannot know yourself and lead yourself out of the wilderness when you have gone astray, you will not be able to lead others. Take care of yourself. No promotion or project is worth sacrificing your health or well-being over it. You want to enjoy your success, not be consumed by it.

Coda: The hydraulic system that caused so many problems and eventually pushed me over the edge? The mechanics ended up simply disabling it until a team of technicians came out several months later and permanently fixed it. I had put myself through this episode for nothing, as is often the case with stress and frustration. A bonus lesson to keep in mind.

REFERENCES

Klug, K., Felfe, J., & Krick, A. (2022). Does self-care make you a better leader? A multisource study linking leader self-care to health-oriented leadership, employee self-care, and health. *International Journal of Environmental Research and Public Health, 19*(11), 6733. https://doi.org/10.3390/ijerph19116733

McArthur, H. V. (2024, December 30). *The skill of self-care: A leadership competency for the modern era.* Forbes. www.forbes.com/sites/hvmacarthur/2024/12/30/the-skill-of-self-care-a-leadership-competency-for-the-modern-era/

Neale, P. (2024, September 27). *A self-care checklist for leaders.* Harvard Business Review. https://hbr.org/2024/09/a-self-care-checklist-for-leaders

Chapter 5

Self-care and personal growth

Take an excursion, get some perspective, use your head in a new or different way

One of the best ways to prevent burnout is simply to take a break. As I said in the last chapter, two weeks in London with my wife turned out to be exactly what I needed. I forced myself to ignore work and focus on exploring something new.

An excursion does not, necessarily, need to be anything extravagant. I had one employee who, on occasion, would simply take a single day of leave as a "mental health day." This employee would use the time to run errands or take care of personal business, so she did not have to worry about these things on the weekend. Hey, the work was getting done, she had the leave, and she arranged it when nothing was pressing on the schedule. As a supervisor, I had no problem in allowing her to do this.

Similarly, in my mid-level 2 assignment, we were not far from the beach, about 30–45 minutes depending on traffic. One of my employees liked to surf, so he went a couple of mornings a week to watch the sunrise over the ocean and catch some waves. When he did this, he got to work a little later than normal. And? My theory is, so what? Normally he gets in earlier than everyone else and is easily as productive, in many cases more productive than others. Yes, I could come down on him and say the rules state he needs to be at his desk at a certain time, but unless his absence for half an hour, a couple of mornings a week causes a problem, then I have no problem. One of the reasons he is so productive is because he had this time to, as he phrases it, "re-center and reenergize" his "chi."

Other people need to go work out at lunch or after the workday is done. There were times in my career when I found time to do yoga (which has been great for my back and why I started in the first place), go for a walk or run, or jump on a bike for 40 minutes. All of this helped with my stress levels and increased my overall energy and productivity.

As an aside, I recommend everyone read "The Making of a Corporate Athlete", published in *Harvard Business Review* (Loehr and Schwartz, 2001). In this report, the authors, Jim Loehr and Tony Schwartz, discuss the "Ideal Performance State" and explain how they have used their experience

DOI: 10.1201/9781003650454-7

working with professional athletes to train corporate executives to be more efficient and productive. As the authors explain, "chronic stress without recovery depletes energy reserves, leads to burnout and breakdown, and ultimately undermines performance." Loehr and Schwartz describe what they call "the high-performance pyramid," which starts with a base of physical capacity and then moves up through levels of emotional capacity, mental capacity, and spiritual capacity, and give examples of executives who made small changes leading to big impacts at the various levels. As they conclude:

> On the playing field or in the boardroom, high performance depends as much on how people renew and recover their energy as on how they expend it, on how they manage their lives as much as on how they manage their work. When people feel strong and resilient—physically, mentally, emotionally, and spiritually—they perform better, with more passion, for longer. They win, their families win, and the corporations that employ them win.
>
> Loehr and Schwartz, 2001

Establishing new rituals and focusing on simple recovery strategies can make a world of difference, reducing overall stress levels and increasing productivity. Sometimes, though, this is not enough, and you need a change of scenery.

One of the reasons I enjoyed working in the DC metro area is that there are so many things to do within a couple of hours' drive. My family and I would often go down to Williamsburg, Virginia, for the weekend and stay at a time-share resort that we have there. Just a quick two-and-a-half- or three-day weekend to change scenery, relax, play some miniature golf with my son, swim in the pool, explore Colonial Williamsburg, or something like that. Alternatively, we sometimes went to the Shenandoah Valley to drive part of the Blue Ridge Parkway or hike some of the wonderful trails. Sometimes, if we only had a day or an afternoon, it was enough simply to go to one of the local parks in Fairfax County to hike, bike, play mini golf, or ride the little train or the merry-go-round with the kids. The point is to take somean excursion, get a change of scenery, and break up the routine.

Because my job moves me around every couple of years, my wife and I have taken to planning "adventures" to go and see different parts of the country (and surrounding countries) where we happen to be. It was during these times that I appreciated my job the most. Yes, work can be interesting and rewarding, but we love to go out and go see things and experience the area where we happen to be living. As Ferris Bueller says, "Life moves pretty fast. If you don't stop and look around once in a while, you could miss it."

When all is said and done, what do you want memories of: your office walls or adventures you had with people with whom you enjoy spending time?

So far, I have mostly focused on personal excursions, but there are professional excursions as well. If these are available to you, don't pass them up.

In my agency, it is sometimes possible to take temporary duty assignments, either for a few days or even several weeks. These opportunities give you a couple of benefits: you get to see a different part of your agency or another agency, you get to see another part of the country or even the world, and you get to experience different leadership styles, which helps you develop your own. You can also sometimes combine official excursions with personal ones: I don't think I would ever have learned to surf in Maui if I had not had a work trip to Honolulu.

There is another kind of opportunity that I highly recommend, especially if you are looking for a change of professional scenery or pace: excursion tours or details to another agency. How this effects your promotability will vary greatly from agency to agency (some agencies require an excursion tour in order for an employee to be promotable; others frown on their employees going "outside the system"). Also, private sector companies sometimes allow this. For instance, a friend of mine was a journalist for a major newspaper and, while still employed there, spent a year as a fellow at a think tank. You need to check with your own agency or company to find out what the policies and possibilities are, but if you feel you are stuck in a rut or are approaching burnout, an excursion may be just what you need to get yourself back on track.

As I was wrapping up my mid-level 1 assignment, I was suddenly confronted with a situation in which I needed to find a one-year tour. My original plans to bid for overseas posts were disrupted as I had a family member with a health issue, and I needed to stay local as the situation resolved. I spoke with several of my mentors to try to see what the options were and started looking over the bidding announcements.

As it turns out, my agency offers several educational opportunities as one-year assignments. I had always wanted to get a master's degree, but I was not sure that I would be successful if I was only working on it part-time while trying to juggle a full-time job and family responsibilities. Here was the perfect opportunity: I could take a year out of the regular hustle and bustle of my agency, and my whole job was to focus on getting a master's degree through this program.

Yes, this was a compressed program, but it was also a well-regarded program that is both fully accredited and a member of the Washington Consortium of Higher Education. In addition to the class load, the program required a thesis reviewed and approved by a panel comprising the thesis adviser and outside readers. This was a serious academic program.

While it was a serious program and a LOT of work, especially reading, it also had much more flexible hours than the typical workday and, much more importantly, allowed me to use my brain differently for the year. The academic work of reading, researching, and writing played perfectly into my INTJ personality. My classmates were intelligent and engaging, and the professors were very good and often were experienced professionals in the fields in which they taught, in addition to having academic credentials.

Each Monday a guest speaker would visit the class and speak about a different topic and offer the opportunity to ask questions. The guest speakers were typically either high-level members of the US national security apparatus or were highly respected journalists and/or members of academia from other institutions. It was a great year, and I had almost passed it up.

As a bright shining rising star in my agency (at least in my own mind), I saw nothing but success ahead of me. Sure, I wanted a master's degree, but I was not going to settle for some random one. I wanted "the show" as they say in baseball. I wanted the major leagues. I wanted either Princeton, Georgetown, or my true goal, the National War College.

The problem with those programs, though, is that you have to be a certain rank to apply for them, and they are very competitive, with many applicants for the few coveted spots each year. I finally realized I was letting my ego get in the way of what I needed. So, when I was confronted by this situation where I needed a one-year tour, I started to look around, and it turned out that there was this program, at my current grade, focused on my field, that looked really interesting. I made some calls and discovered the application deadline had not yet passed, and luckily, I was selected for admission.

So, what if you already have a master's degree? Get another. Many companies have programs that allow you to take university courses either for free or through a reimbursement program. Maybe your agency or company does not offer this kind of program. If not, they probably offer training opportunities. Perhaps it will only be for a couple of days or weeks, but it is a chance to get out and use your brain in a different way and gain some perspective. If your agency or company offers no academic programs and no training opportunities, then go find something on your own time.

One of the best things that I got out of this program, other than the diploma, was the perspective. When you get into a bureaucracy, and you start moving up the reporting chain, you tend to focus on the next step up the chain, but not a lot further. You may get tunnel vision and start to see your career in the company or agency without recognizing that there is more out there. One of the things this academic program did for me was broaden my perspective. It allowed me to see other paths I could take, both inside and outside my agency. This gave me back a sense of control over my destiny.

One advantage of my master's degree excursion year was that I figured this out halfway through my career. This was an advantage because I was able to hedge my career bets, work to get promoted, and if I reached a certain level, I could choose to stay on a couple of years past retirement eligibility. But, if I saw that it was not working out as I hoped, then I could also work to shape my career to give me the most advantages to permanently punch the time clock and check out at the first opportunity.

I have had a lot of friends and colleagues at work who were nearing their own retirement. Some of them were clawing and scratching to get every single minute they could out of their career, because they had no idea what else they would do. Others had found a passion outside of the job and couldn't wait to retire so they could focus on their passion. In speaking with the ones who were desperately hanging on, the common response as to why they were doing so was not financial; instead, it was a sense that they had no idea what else they would do.

I came across this so often, I wrote an article titled "Always Remember, You Are More," published on Medium.com. (Stitt, 2021). As I stated in the article, "If what you are doing energizes you each day and imbues you with a sense of passion, great! Stick with it. But if you feel frustration and dread when you look at your life and think of your identity and how it is linked to a profession, maybe it is time to break that chain and look at reinventing yourself." I conclude the article, saying, "No matter what, at some point, the music stops, the merry-go-round ride ends, and you need to go find another ride. Isn't it better to already have a sense of what you want to do next?"

Even before leaving government service, I found an opportunity to throw myself back into academia as an adjunct faculty member at a university in the Washington, DC, area. Again, I enjoy the process of research and writing that goes into course design. I really enjoy reading the discussion board posts and other interactions with the students as I see their learning take place.

Since leaving government service, I have taken more opportunities for personal enrichment, including completing two programs through the Institute of Presilience®, which is based in Australia. The Graduate Certificate in Organizational Resilience, Risk, and High Reliability and the Graduate Diploma in Organizational Presilience, Risk, and High Performance are deep dives into the Presilience framework and methodology.

Preslience is more than simply proactive resilience. It focuses on the combination of factors in leadership, the psychology of risk, high performance, principles of high-reliability organizations, team dynamics, and more to help people and organizations drive with high performance during business as usual and thrive in disruption. The CEO of the Institute of Presilience, Gavriel Schneider, published a book on the foundational concepts in 2025 (Schneider, 2025).

One of the concepts embedded in Presilience is the "whole of person model." According to Jai Chaggar, "The approach focuses on nurturing the physical, emotional, mental, and spiritual aspects of an employee's life" (Chaggar, 2024). Many sources trace the origins of the concepts to traditional Indian and Chinese medicine, and the principles have been embraced by modern health care and organizational development leaders. It is a recognition that the whole person needs care, including self-care. To lead yourself, and then others and organizations, you need to invest in self-care and personal growth. Maybe that starts with an excursion out of your daily routine.

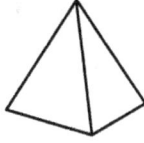

Here is the lesson:
Take an excursion, gain some perspective, use your head in a different way. Depending on the circumstances of what you need and what you can get, this can be a 40-minute workout, an afternoon off, a long weekend, a couple of weeks' vacation, or a year in a different kind of job. This helps prevent burnout and helps you recognize the world outside your cubicle or office and that there might actually be other things in that world that you want to do.

REFERENCES

Chaggar, J. (2024, February). Embracing the whole person approach in organizational development. Together. www.togetherplatform.com/blog/embracing-the-whole-person-approach-in-organizational-development#:~:text=Overview%20of%20the%20whole%2Dperson%20approach&text=The%20approach%20focuses%20on%20nurturing,and%20experiences%20to%20drive%20innovation.

Loehr, J., & Schwartz, T. (2001, January). *The making of a corporate athlete.* Harvard Business Review. https://hbr.org/2001/01/the-making-of-a-corporate-athlete

Schneider, G. (2025). *Presilience: How to navigate risk, embrace opportunity, and build resilience.* Amplify Publishing.

Stitt, C. (2021, April 9). Always remember, you are more. Medium.com. https://medium.com/p/3e66f414b575

Chapter 6

Manage your followership style

Change is constant; even in the same organization you still need to adjust

In my Journeyman 2 assignment, relatively early in my career, I had incredible freedom to run the program as I saw fit and possessed easy access to the upper levels of my bureaucracy. The program itself had a government-wide and global impact (not exaggerating, I shared part of my annual review in Chapter 3), and I admit, I felt an awful lot as if I were king of the world, my world at least.

Then my career went ... sideways, and it took some time to recover from the change.

As I have mentioned, one of the great benefits of life in my agency, and to some extent one of the curses, is that we rotate jobs frequently. My tenure in Journeyman 2 was two years. As I mentioned, in this assignment, I was the BOSS: I was leading a major Pyramid-wide change effort, which is a little crazy considering my short length of overall tenure and low rank. While I still had people to answer to, I held a lot of authority and responsibility and direct contact with people throughout the Department of Pyramids, most of them several ranks higher than I was.

When my two years were up, I asked to extend, but I was told that it would not be "career enhancing," so I was forced to rotate to a new position. I clearly remember the moment at which I felt my career go sideways. I was walking out of our office building to go and grab a cup of coffee when the principal deputy assistant secretary of my bureau (PDAS, this is similar to the vice president for operations, check the graphic in the introduction for a refresher) approached me on the sidewalk and said, "Chris, walk with me for a minute. We need to talk about what you are going to do next."

This guy was a good leader, and I have a lot of respect for him. Plus, I was relatively young and early in my career, so when someone of this level pays attention to you and wants to talk to you about what career track you should follow, you should pay attention, which is what I did.

See, I already had an idea in mind of what I wanted to do next. Since I had already been told that I would be unable to extend, I had talked to a couple of people about where I should go. As the conversation with the

DOI: 10.1201/9781003650454-8

PDAS started, I thought maybe someone had mentioned to him what my aspirations were. As I noted in Chapter 3, I have something of a knack for understanding how people interact with computer systems. I had even had conversations with the chief technology officer (CTO) about creating a position for me in which I would be the bridge between the offices that needed applications to be developed and the developers who wrote the code because I could translate pretty well between the two cultures. I was really looking forward to this opportunity because I would still have a lot of freedom, would be pioneering a new concept and position in my agency, and would still have a lot of access to the upper levels of the bureaucracy.

So, I was really shocked when the PDAS said, "Chris, the current CTO is retiring, the position you were hoping for is not going to be possible. You need to think about other options." He went on to explain that I had a lot of potential—yeah, great—but that I needed to make sure I had a well-rounded career to ensure I was competitive to be promoted across the threshold into the senior ranks of my agency. "So," he said, "I think you should go" in a completely different direction. He could tell I was not enthusiastic about the idea, but he encouraged me to talk to a couple of people.

One of those people I knew pretty well, as he had overseen the first office I worked in for my entry-level 1 assignment. He was now the head of domestic operations for my bureau. He explained that he wanted me to work in a particular office because he thought my skill set would be useful as they tried to modernize their operations. Plus, I would be a supervisor, which would be good for my career. While I had supervised people in my Journeyman-2 assignment, they were all contractors, so they did not count under my agency's philosophy of responsible supervision. In this new job, I would supervise other direct-hire employees, to develop those skills. He encouraged me to talk to the head of the office in question.

I went to talk to the head of the office, and we hit it off well. He had some ideas of how I could be productive and useful, supervising one of the units in the office, and working on some special projects he was trying to accomplish. It also offered me a chance to gain a new skill set due to the unique nature of the office's mandate. Though I was wary and still very attached to my then-current assignment, I decided that this was probably my best option, so I took it.

Now, remember how I got here: I was approached by the PDAS on the street because he wanted to talk about my future; I then went to talk to the director of domestic operations, who falls right under the PDAS; and I then went to the head of the office where I ended up working. Instead of working my way up the pyramid to get this job, through fate and circumstance, I started at the top of the pyramid and worked my way down. This is not how it usually works. Typically, when we rotate, we start by lobbying the person we want to replace and then work our way up. Even though I was still wary of this new job since it was not what I dreamed of, I still felt pretty special.

From a professional and personal standpoint, this assignment was one of the hardest.

I walked into a situation where I was supervising not one but two disgruntled employees, along with three others who were high performers. Also, very early in my tenure in the new office, I easily accomplished a task that had been challenging one of the other unit supervisors, and he became rather hostile toward me because he felt I had made him look bad. I had not intended to make him look bad. It just so happened that I had the right combination of contacts from my previous assignment to get the task done quickly and easily.

Moreover, I now had an immediate supervisor who liked to play games with information, claiming "need to know" privileges and ensuring that all contact with higher levels of management, including and especially people at the level I had dealt with to get the job, went through him. And by through him, I mean that I reported to him, and he reported information up the pyramid himself. We were to have very limited, or preferably no, contact with higher levels of management.

I'll discuss in later chapters about handling problem employees and the leadership lessons I learned from my new boss. The point of this story, however, concerns how I adjusted. See, you cannot expect a situation to adjust to you; instead, you need to adjust to the situation. Followership is an important bedrock for leadership.

This is not a new concept. In fact, many sources attribute the following words to the ancient Greek philosopher Aristotle: "He who cannot be a good follower cannot be a good leader." Originally appearing in Aristotle's *Politics* as "He who has never learned to obey cannot be a good commander" (Aristotle, 1998), the original words, and the contemporary paraphrase that encapsulates it, can be found quite frequently in a Google search. It is used by such diverse sources as leadership development authors and trainers, and even the Association of the United States Army has an article on the topic. Recent research bears this out as well.

In a 2018 study, Kim Peters and Alex Haslam examined a recruit class of Royal Marines to gauge their emergent leadership traits. As the authors summarized in a *Harvard Business Review* article on their study, it was "the recruits who saw themselves (and were seen by commanders) as followers who ultimately emerged as leaders. In other words, it seems that those who want to lead are well served by first endeavoring to follow" (Peters and Haslam, 2018). In order to lead a group of people, it helps to be seen as part of that group, not separate from it. In this vein, this mid-level 1 assignment was a huge personal learning experience for me, even more than a professional learning experience.

First, I realized I would not have the freedom I had enjoyed in my previous assignment. I needed to adjust to the new structure. After a couple of weeks, I felt like I was getting the hang of things in the new office, but I also felt like I was still missing something, some key that would allow me to decode or unlock this new job to help me feel truly successful. So, I looked around the office, found another unit supervisor who had been in the office for almost two years, and took her to lunch. Over lunch, I explained my feelings and concerns and asked for her advice.

This was helpful. This supervisor explained how I had frustrated our colleague and how I had come in, full of energy and ego, and rubbed some people the wrong way, especially because of how the office operated. It had a much more stoic culture: focused on process, procedure, and slowly, meticulously assembled reports and other information products. As I mentioned in Chapter 3, my personality is bent the other way: leaps of logic, intuitive thinking, here's what we need to do, let's go. This was not a pace or method that others in the office were comfortable with.

With this advice, I started to make some changes in how I operated. I tried to keep my ego in check and adapt to how the office ran instead of hoping I could energize it and adapt it to me. This was not easy, but it gave me some perspective, and I focused my energy on other aspects of the job, learning as much as I could. I offered assistance to other units in the office and found a couple of areas in which my particular expertise was warmly welcomed.

One of the units needed a better way to track the metrics they were gathering so they could report the numbers to help show the value of their efforts. I produced a relatively simple spreadsheet with embedded graphs that created a concise yet powerful report to help them get their point across. They then used this tool for several years to successfully defend their program and advocate for resources.

I also worked with the unit in charge of creating policy for the topic we covered. This helped me sate my curiosity and desire to learn, while at the same time giving me tremendous insight into the history and reasoning of "why" certain programs worked the way they did.

In my own unit, I took the opportunity to focus on the nuts and bolts of supervision. I tried to work with the employees to give them projects they were interested in and shift responsibilities around to help them out. It worked well, and one of my problem employees became a great asset.

Then, after my first year in the assignment, it changed again. This time for the better. A good friend rotated in to replace the unit supervisor who did not like me. We also got a new office director. While both changes were welcome, I still had a relationship with my immediate supervisor that ran hot and cold. Sometimes I seemed to be in his good graces and other times I was on the outside looking in. The second year in the assignment was better, but frankly, I never felt I truly adjusted. In fact, just as I really felt I was getting into the swing of things and had acclimated to the environment, it was time to rotate again. This time, though, I was going for something completely different: a master's degree.

I spoke about the excursion tour in the last chapter, but for the purposes of this chapter, I will simply say that sometimes, change can be good, even great! Moving back into an academic environment, especially one that was as high caliber as this one, was a very welcome change: a chance to use my head in a different way. My wife tells me that she had never seen me happier or more balanced than I was during that year. It is probably true. It was a great change and a fabulous year, but in the end, I was ready to get back to my real job.

Unfortunately, because of budget issues, the project I had originally been assigned to undertake following my master's degree was delayed for a year, so I needed to find something else. The only thing available at my grade was a deputy job. I did not want to be a deputy. I wanted to get back to running a program and get myself back on the pace that I felt had been rudely interrupted by fate that day on the street as I went to get coffee. But a deputy I was destined to be.

Again, I needed to adjust. My first boss in my mid-level 2 assignment was a pretty good guy, but he was at times very frustrating to work for. As a leader, he had a lot of knowledge and was good at sharing it, making sure that all the people in the office had the opportunity to learn, and he rotated taking me and the other staff to various meetings to ensure we had the exposure we needed to understand the job better and prepare us for higher levels of responsibility.

But I tell you, the guy could play head games. He would drop a comment just to see how people would react. He would use a tone of voice that you weren't sure if he was serious or not. It could be incredibly frustrating because you were never really certain where you stood with him, receiving respect or contempt. He was also intensely private, not wanting to be a target of workplace gossip, which, of course, for some people increased their inquisitiveness and desire to gossip about him. Also, he was a very active guy who took care of a lot of the routine business himself, sometimes leaving the rest of us wondering what we were supposed to be doing.

In the end, it worked out and we were quite productive together. Part of that was that I worked to adjust my followership style to his leadership style and in many ways, our differing strengths complemented each other.

Then, he rotated out.

I had been hoping beyond hope that I would be able to get out from under the deputy title and possibly get the bump to run the office myself.

In an effort to move up the pyramid, I reached out to a friend who was now very senior in my bureau ... and was rebuffed. I was told that it was highly unlikely I would get the job. Such is life. I had accepted the deputy position; I would stick it out.

But then, like a sign from God, clouds parting and angels singing, the person selected to replace my boss broke his assignment for family reasons. It turns out, I misread the sign. Even though I had assurances from my senior-level friend, someone else got the assignment.

My next problem was, I had no idea who had gotten the job. I called my friend, and she told me she was unsure because she had been traveling when the decision was made. That was on a Friday. On Monday, one of my team members called me. He had just heard from a friend in another city about who the person coming in was. Fortunately, it was someone I had worked with before, so at least I knew him. Unfortunately, this person was the same rank as I and had only been on the job a year longer. Concerningly, the contact who had called did not have an overly favorable opinion of the person, or his leadership style.

Ready, set, shift. Anytime there is a change, you need to decide: try to adapt—or leave. Quite frankly, I looked around and examined a couple of exits, but for a variety of reasons, mostly family based, I chose to stay. Two of my team members started looking hard for a way out and took it when they found it. I fully understood and supported their desire to move on; it was good for both them and the office because their frustration level with the situation was growing and apparent. I was sticking it out.

My new supervisor arrived, and the rumors about his leadership style were true. He was a very hands-off kind of supervisor, but he made sure that he was the face and voice of the office up the pyramid. I had gone from one extreme, a supervisor who did almost everything, leaving the rest of us wondering what we were supposed to do, to a supervisor who did almost nothing but allowed us the freedom to run our projects more independently.

With the departure of my two subordinates came the arrival of two new ones. One came in with some great experience and the skills to run his own office. The other was newer to the job but smart and motivated to learn. Between the three of us, we managed to easily run the day-to-day operations, freeing up our boss to take on the outside liaison activities and higher-level meetings. Again, this all took some adjustment, but luckily the personalities that came in meshed well and the two new team members were good at adapting their followership styles, which made the adjustment easier.

The new boss presented several challenges that I will use as examples in later chapters. In the end, I survived the assignment and learned a lot, because I was able to adapt my followership style.

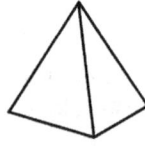

Here is the lesson:
The ability to lead yourself to adapt your followership style to chan-
ging leadership styles is critical for success. You need to keep your
ego in check, and even in a difficult situation, focus on what you can
learn and accomplish. Find ways to support the mission of the work
unit and make the needed adjustments.

REFERENCES

Aristotle. (1998). *Politics* (C. D. C. Reeve, Trans.). Hackett Publishing Company. (Original work produced ca 350 BCE). https://classics.mit.edu/Aristotle/politics.3.three.html

Peters, K., & Haslam, A. (2018, August). *Research: To be a good leader, start by being a good follower*. Harvard Business Review. https://hbr.org/2018/08/research-to-be-a-good-leader-start-by-being-a-good-follower

Chapter 7

Managing impressions
How do others see you?

A man I know, when asked the key to success in our bureaucracy, used to reply, "Start slowly, then taper off." It's a funny saying, and it is pretty descriptive of the way many people view bureaucrats. This brings up a good point: how do others see you? I previously discussed understanding your strengths and weaknesses in Chapter 3. It is one thing to be able to describe yourself, but another thing altogether to understand how others see you.

One of the comments I get often is "Why aren't you an IT guy? You have a real gift for computer systems." Frankly, I like technology (you probably noticed that in Chapter 3), but one of the things I love about my job (then and now) is the variety and the adventure. I work with technology because I enjoy it, but I think if I were forced to focus on that full-time, I would quickly burn out.

Therefore, I explain that while I am good at navigating computer systems, exploring applications, and I enjoy the new challenges they constantly present, there are other parts of my job I like more.

I get a little frustrated at this pigeonholing, though. Yes, I am good at figuring out technological applications, but my expertise is much broader than that. In fact, one of the things I am actually pretty good at is technology/process integration. Being able to navigate computer systems is not enough. To be good at technology/process integration, you must be able to see the big picture of what the policy is attempting to achieve and the processes in use to reach the policy goals (making sure the tactical and strategic are aligned). Once you understand that, then you can start looking at how to use technology to combine or skip steps. The goal is not to change the policy to suit the technology; rather, the goal is to find technology to support the policy. This is a much more complex challenge than simply showing someone how to turn on and off the bold text feature in a word processing program. The problem is getting people to see this side of me so they don't simply write me off as "the office computer guy."

Part of this is how you brand yourself. During my mid-level 2 assignment, a senior official from another division of my local pyramid offered to put me

DOI: 10.1201/9781003650454-9

in for an award for all the work I did on a project that really let me stretch my computer skills. The problem was the person was having trouble capturing in words what I had accomplished because he was focused simply on the technological side: the product that he saw. Once I put it into terms of technology/process integration and explained the behind-the-scenes mental gymnastics I had performed to come up with my technological solutions, it was like a light bulb went off: he had never thought of it in that context before and he used that to write the award. Developing this personal brand of an innovative integrator of policy, process, and technology helped lead to additional opportunities throughout my career.

Other factors feed into how people perceive you. Some of it is physical. People will make snap judgments about you based on how you look: tall, short, slender, heavy, and so forth. Some of that you cannot control. But there are other things you can control: how you carry yourself, how you dress, what your demeanor is, what your attitude is like.

As I mentioned earlier, it is one thing to say, "describe yourself." It is quite another to ask yourself, "how would others describe you?" Would the answers match? Do you have any ideas?

One of the ways my agency tried to help with this is called the 360 review. My agency uses this technique pretty heavily, especially as an employee attempts to obtain more competitive jobs. A résumé is one-sided, as is a personal bio; you tweak these things to make yourself look good and highlight your strengths. A 360 is exactly what it sounds like: the people in charge of choosing the candidate send questionnaires to your supervisor, to at least one colleague, and if you are a supervisor, to at least one of your subordinates. They look at you from all sides, 360 degrees. Now, there is still a little bit of fallacy in this because you nominate who you want the surveys sent to, but it is still a much different process than simply sending in a résumé.

Some of the 360 evaluations I have been asked to participate in have been very formal and structured, with rating scales for various traits. These are usually supplemented by comment boxes so you can explain your answers. Other 360 evaluations I have received have been unstructured with a short list of questions that you respond to in free-form text, kind of to give a thumbnail sketch of your opinion of the candidate.

While the 360s have not been fully standardized and vary somewhat, one of the better ones that I was asked to complete on one of my former team members contained the following questions:

1. How well does the candidate work with others, i.e., superiors, peers, and subordinates?
2. How would you rate the candidate's leadership skills, promotion of diversity, ability to delegate work, and ability to inspire good performance?

3. Do you believe that the candidate exercises good judgment? If you had a job-related problem, would you seek his/her advice?

4. Please rate the candidate's communications skills. Are instructions/guidelines clear? Are subordinates' concerns and ideas taken into consideration?

5. Has the candidate demonstrated people leadership skills, including an interest in mentoring more junior employees? Does the candidate proactively supervise subordinates providing regular, clear, and useful feedback and guidance on how to improve their performance? Does the candidate give due attention and diligence to evaluating supervisees, particularly through the annual Employee Evaluation Report?

6. If you were writing the candidate's evaluation, what would you likely suggest as an area or skill to focus on strengthening? In your experience, how has the candidate responded to criticism?

Normally, if you are the subject of a 360 review, you never see what the responses are. However, one of the interesting things about the leadership training that my agency requires is that every level has a 360. You are required to send a survey to a certain number of people (minimum ten), and the responses are combined into a report, making it harder (not always impossible) to figure out who said what. This is actually a very useful tool, if (a big if) you can convince people to be honest in their answers. This lets you know how you are actually perceived, at least from the standpoint of your leadership style and capability. The odds are good that the 360 you get as part of training will be pretty similar to the answers an assignments selection committee will get when you are bidding on an onward assignment.

Research bears this out. Morgan Massie, in an article published by *Forbes*, highlights the utility of 360 evaluations and several studies that reinforce this idea. One of her points is that 360 feedback is most effective when it comes from a variety of sources to ensure a holistic view of a leader's strengths and areas for improvement. (Massie, 2023).

Some authors highlight that caution is needed when implementing a 360-review process. There is a danger of toxic feedback from disgruntled respondents. As Meg Halverson details in her *New York Times* article "360 Reviews Often Lead to Cruel, Not Constructive, Criticism," she has seen plentiful examples in her management consulting practice of people using the process simply to troll the subject of the review. In some cases, this was based on petty jealousies or personality clashes, but she also highlights that different dynamics may be at play when 360 reviews are used for competitive promotions. As she explains, "Peers may be envious and wish to cause damage. Managers may want to demonstrate their own superiority. And people who report to the person being reviewed may have an ax to grind over any number of workplace issues" (Halverson, 2016).

For me, the results of the 360 reports I received as part of leadership training generally aligned with how I saw myself, but there were certainly insights that surprised me and helped me identify areas to work on. Without these reports and colleagues who were kind enough to be honest in their responses, I would never have recognized some of my blind spots. Luckily, I was not subjected to the toxic trolling identified by Halverson.

While my department implemented the 360 process more strongly each year in the assignment selection process, one area where they have not implemented it yet is the promotion process. There has actually been a lot of talk about doing this though. Imagine for a minute what your organization would be like if promotions were based, at least partially, on how good a manager and leader your subordinates and colleagues report you are, rather than just how your bosses rate and review you. In my department, it would be a major game changer.

Another method to get feedback is simply to ask people. Halverson recommends making a habit of routinely asking for feedback after meetings, interviews, and tough conversations. This is a habit that I got into later in my career and still use to this day. There are times when I want to make sure the tone and delivery of a point I am trying to make match the goal of the point. So, I ask one or more of the recipients for their impressions. This has helped me fine-tune my approach and messaging in high-stakes conversations. Also, at one point, my department incorporated a mini-360 into mid-year counseling sessions. Supervisors were encouraged to ask their subordinates about how the supervisor was doing in supporting the subordinates and if there were any areas in which the supervisor could improve. I felt this was a good strategy, but as you may imagine, many employees were uncomfortable giving honest feedback in these conversations. The department dropped this from the mid-year counseling session requirements after about two years.

I kept this practice, though, and even expanded it into part of my routine interactions with my team, asking how I could support them better, whether there was anything they needed from me, and in what ways I could adjust my leadership style to better fit their followership style. Then, when it came time for the mid-year reviews, the conversations were more comfortable and open, because my team members knew I was honestly seeking feedback. It was interesting to get feedback. I remember one employee who felt I was micromanaging on certain topics, and another employee who appreciated and even desired the more explicit direction and support on those same topics. I was able to make the necessary changes for each of them, but I would never have known unless I had asked and developed a reputation as a leader who appreciated feedback.

Even if your agency or company does not use a formal process like a 360 review, there is still another concept that you need to be aware of: the hallway reputation.

When I started with the Department of Pyramids and I was in my initial training, one of the things that the class coordinator stressed was the need to manage your "hallway reputation." Literally, what do people say about you behind your back when they talk while walking down the hallway. In my department, this is HUGE. Even with the new emphasis on the more formal 360 process, the hallway reputation is still a major factor in which jobs you get and how you are received when you get there.

Remember what I said in the last chapter about the rumors we heard about my new supervisor? Opinions were formed and people started to make decisions about staying or leaving before the person even arrived, without even giving him a chance. Maybe it is unfair, but the hallway reputation is a reality. Further, the broader based the consensus is and the more similar the descriptions are from a wider range of people, the more likely the reputation is to be accurate.

The only way to change your hallway reputation, or determine whether you need to change it, is to find out what it is. This starts with a brave decision to ask trusted confidants to be honest with you. This can be incredibly hard to face, especially if the result is that your image of yourself is quite different from the image others have of you.

Another method, as recommended by Rob McKenna in his book *Composed: The Heart and Science of Leading under Pressure*," is to develop a trusted board of personal advisers. As he writes in the chapter on self-awareness, "They may be close friends or family members, colleagues at work, mentors or managers, but they are all invested in you and being honest with you. Keep in mind that the intention is to increase your self-awareness. Don't hesitate to make that clear to your board of advisors" (McKenna, 2017, p. 72).

I have developed an informal board of personal advisers, especially as I transitioned out of government service and into the private sector. Recently, one of those advisers started to encourage me to formalize this group, introduce my advisers to each other, and even set up a monthly call. Part of this strategy is for business development, but a core aspect is also personal development. Feedback from a variety of people who are invested in your success can be incredibly powerful.

Knowing is the first step to making the necessary improvements to be a stronger leader. This is why I like the mandatory 360 process that is part of my agency's leadership training: it forces you to listen to the Greek chorus that is giving the narrative. It is also why I make a habit of asking for feedback and have developed a network of trusted advisers to help me continue to improve.

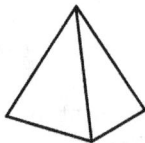

Here is the lesson:
How are you viewed by others? Do you know? You need to find out.
We all have opinions about ourselves, but the opinions of others do
matter. Knowing their opinions can help you improve as a leader.

REFERENCES

Halverson, M. (2016, February 28). *360 reviews often lead to cruel, not constructive, criticism.* New York Times. www.nytimes.com/2016/02/28/jobs/360-reviews-often-lead-to-cruel-not-constructive-criticism.html

Massie, M. (2023, October 26). *Unlocking leadership growth: The power of 360-degree feedback.* Forbes. www.forbes.com/councils/forbescoachescouncil/2023/10/26/unlocking-leadership-growth-the-power-of-360-degree-feedback/

McKenna, R. (2017). *Composed: The art and science of leading under pressure.* Dustjacket Books.

Part II

Leading others

Leading yourself is great; being able to lead others is even better. There is a tremendous difference between "supervising," "managing," and "leading."

Supervising usually entails doling out work requirements, overseeing the work, ensuring it's done, and writing the performance evaluation. Managing takes supervising to a more complex level, bringing together disparate parts to form a cohesive group to accomplish a goal. Managing often entails smoothing out friction points between various personalities, and shepherding the group to keep them on target. Leading is about inspiring others to follow you, to want to work for you, and to want to chase after the goal that you set.

Throughout my assignments captured in this book, I had about 20 supervisors and managers. I would not qualify all of them as leaders. They may have believed they were the leaders of the organizational units they oversaw, but some often failed to exhibit the qualities to make themselves true leaders.

That said, some of these supervisors and managers exhibited one or more leadership qualities, and a couple of them had the whole package, individuals I would follow anywhere. These are the ones that if they were to call me tomorrow and say, "Hey, I have a project (or position) and I want you to come work on it," I would have very little hesitation in saying, "Let me check the flight schedule, I'm on my way."

This is another interesting facet of my department. As I said in the introduction, we rotate jobs frequently, usually every two to three years. One thing this means is that if you are going to establish yourself as a leader and build your reputation that way, you need to do it quickly. Otherwise, people may do the minimum just to get by and wait until they rotate out or you do, or if you or your reputation is bad enough, they will start looking for an exit even before you arrive. Either way, this is very disruptive to the achievement of your goals, and the organization's goals.

DOI: 10.1201/9781003650454-10

As you read these next chapters, again reflect on the anecdotes and try to determine where you see yourself along the spectrum of leadership. Read and reflect on the lessons at the end of each chapter. The goal is to move from simply supervising or managing people, to becoming a leader who inspires others to follow you.

Chapter 8

Differentiating motivations

Employees are like snowflakes, no two are the same

In elementary school, we are all told that no two people are the same. Like snowflakes, we are all unique. There has been a major effort, though, to catalog and categorize "types." I discussed in Chapter 3 my experience with the Myers-Briggs Personality Type Inventory and how learning more about my type has helped me evolve as a leader. There are several other tools that you can use.

One of the most popular is the DiSC Model, which categorizes assessment takers into a combination of personality traits of Dominance, Influence, Steadiness, and Conscientiousness (Everything DiSC, 2023). These are then combined and weighted to give a holistic report that provides insights into the assessment takers' preferences and tendencies, categorizing them into two primary dimensions, four quadrants, and 12 personality styles. This information can then be used to help people find the right fit of qualities and personalities in the workplace, management, leadership, and even sales.

Another popular model is called the "Big Five." This model is sometimes also called the OCEAN model and is based on a combination of Openness to Experience, Conscientiousness, Extraversion, Agreeableness, and Neuroticism. According to a history of the Big Five by Lewis Goldberg, the research on this framework goes back to the 1930s as psychologists worked to determine various personality attributes and how they interact with each other. Through the 1980s and early 1990s, additional research found the five listed above (Goldberg, 1993). Today, there are many free tests available online to help you determine your Big Five.

One of the best assessments I have found is the Whole and Intentional Leader Development Toolkit by WiLD Leaders. This is a series of ten self-reflective assessments that allow deep dives into topics such as your purpose and calling, your meaningful goals, how you lead under pressure, transformational experiences, skills, knowledge, motivations, how you invest in people, and who invests in you. This culminates in a WiLD Plan to help you identify strategies for improvement (WiLD Leaders, 2025). The tool kit is the work of Rob McKenna, who is often listed as one of the top 30 organizational/industrial psychologists in the world.

Understanding yourself and your own motivations is helpful in developing yourself as a leader, but this part is on leading others. So how do you figure out what motivates the members of your team? Perhaps your agency or company has access to personality testing that is shared with managers (mandatorily or voluntarily). But what if you don't have this? It is not enough to HOPE that employees will follow you. Some may argue that FEAR is the best motivator (I have worked for and been around plenty of "leaders" who believe this); I disagree. In reality, you are not really going to know what motivates your employees unless you ask them.

One of the things my department experimented with was called an "Individual Development Plan." This is NOT a performance development plan. It is really a guided self-reflection where the supervisor and employee talk about the employee's strengths, weaknesses, goals, motivating factors, and so on. This can be revealing. You may believe that you are the best leader and manager in the world and that your employees follow you out of a sense of awe and respect. You may be right, but there is probably something else there too, some other reason the employees are performing, or not performing. The individual development plan process is a good way to get into this and discover more.

I admit that I was skeptical when I first sat down with one of my team members to go through this process. I had been working with this particular group for a little over a year already and we already had a good rapport. However, as I went through the questions with them, I gained more insight and continued to strengthen that rapport.

As I said, the individual development plan is not a performance development plan. It looks at the employee from a broader context as a person (similar to the Whole Person Model I mentioned in Chapter 5). A lot of people may claim that they want to separate their work and personal lives. Frankly, you can rarely separate the two. There is almost always going to be some sort of overlap, mostly because you are one person.[1] By using an individual development plan, you can accomplish two things: find those areas of overlap and develop strategies to mutually reinforce those areas to help the employees develop their personal goals; learn about the employee and strengthen your rapport. You can also discover more about some of the frustrations the employee is experiencing and develop strategies to alleviate them.

Another tool my agency uses is mandatory mid-year counseling sessions. Uh oh, that's right, counseling sessions, where the supervisor calls the employee in, closes the door, and has a "talk." Counseling sessions have a negative connotation because they are usually reserved for when a supervisor perceives an employee has transgressed or is not performing adequately. My department is trying to turn that around by mandating routine counseling sessions, just to talk in general terms about how things are going. As I see it, one of the best questions on the counseling session form is "Are you getting the level of supervision that you need?" Due to the concerns about using the word "counseling" for these sessions, many agencies and companies, instead refer to them as "mid-year reviews."

I cannot think of anyone who actually wants to be micromanaged, but there are employees out there who do want more input and feedback from their supervisor, maybe in general or maybe simply on a particular project. Other employees may feel that you are not giving them the freedom to perform at their best. If you can have an honest, routine conversation with the employees, you may find that you can make small (or large) adjustments that will help the performance of the overall team.

Sometimes, the feedback may not be what you expect or want to hear, but you need to keep an open mind. If you are fair with the employees, they will generally be fair with you. As we moved more and more into a 360-review process, this sort of counseling session was beneficial for both the supervisor and the employee, when we actually followed up and implemented the changes discussed.

This brings us back to motivation. I have found I am often motivated by:

- engaging in projects that I think can have a positive impact to create efficiency,
- learning new things, and
- receiving genuine appreciation for my efforts.

Yes, awards are nice, cash awards even more so, but as you will read in a later chapter on awards, I truly like a sense of genuine appreciation more than a cash award for which I have to write my own nomination.

I have had some employees who require constant feedback to stay motivated, almost like they need a cheering section to keep going. Other employees are motivated simply by new challenges and would rather be left alone while they work out the details. Some employees are motivated by the simple sense of a job well done; they do not seek out the appreciation of others. The point here is that you need to find out what motivates people and then try your best to give them that.

There are at least four ways to determine what motivates people: assume, experiment, analyze, and ask.

Many supervisors make the mistake of simply assuming they know what motivates their employees. The supervisor stereotypes the employee early on and unilaterally decides how they are going to get that employee to perform. This can lead to a lot of frustration for both the employee and the supervisor. Yes, the supervisor may get lucky and hit on what truly motivates that employee. More likely, though, the employee will perform but will not reach his or her full potential, and the supervisor will be just that, someone who supervises, not someone who leads.

The second option is to experiment. In this case, the supervisor will try out different motivational schemes on the employee or group of employees so they can try to determine, through a process of elimination, the best way to motivate the individual or group of employees. We had a senior site manager like this when I was in my mid-level 2 assignment. The saying about him was that you could always tell when he was reading a new management theory book because he would use the workplace as his own experimental lab and try out the techniques to see if they worked for him. While often frustrating due to the constantly changing management style, this was occasionally comical as the changes came across as unnatural, and it was apparent that he was experimenting on us.

The third option is to analyze. You can think about previous interactions, assignments, work products, and so on to infer motivation. For example, if an employee asks to be put up for awards, you can fairly conclude that awards are a motivator. If they had a spark of energy on a certain project or task, you could infer that they were motivated by the topic. If they seem energized (or de-energized) when tasked to work with certain people, you can infer that there is a good (or bad) personality mix.

This brings us to the fourth, and in my estimation best, option, which is to simply ask. Sadly, in my mid-level 2 assignment, I went for two years without a counseling session, though I had asked for them, and my annual evaluation stated I had had four of them. We never even had a conversation about my goals and motivations. My supervisor was of the "assume" mentality. Unfortunately, his assumptions were often wrong. Luckily, as the deputy, I was able to serve as a buffer between him and the rest of the office. I did analyze and ask, which contributed to our section's overall high performance. We had some great people on the team, and by understanding their motivations and helping them understand mine, we achieved some great accomplishments.

I see a certain simple brilliance in the individual development plan and mandatory counseling session mix. It was always interesting to me to get new employees in my office who had been with my agency for several years and I was the first supervisor who took the time to actually do this. At first the reaction was typically, "Why are we wasting time on this? There is work to do." But as the process progressed, there was usually more a sense of "Wow, I never really thought about that," concluding with an increased level of mutual respect. Then,I found that if I actually followed up on the conversations and implemented some of the suggestions, I went from being someone who simply oversaw the employee's work, to someone they respected and would follow. I became their leader.

The motivating factors will be as varied as the employees themselves. I had one employee who told me in our first counseling session that he wanted a certain level of award. Flat out, he told me that he wanted a meritorious pay scale step increase (which leads to a permanent pay increase). He was feeling overlooked and underappreciated. He had a lot of experience and a lot of potential; he wanted the recognition he felt he deserved. I did not promise him the award. I promised that we would set up a plan for him to hit certain benchmarks for me to justify the award. Through the year, he hit the benchmarks, and I made sure he got the award.

Later in my career, I was often asked to take on "disgruntled" employees who other managers could not handle. I found that it was often best to start my introduction to these employees with a request, "Tell me your story." I had this experience frequently enough that I wrote an article on it that was published by WiLD Leaders, "Tell Me Your Story: Recovering the Unled and Mismanaged" (Stitt, 2021). I found that many of these "disgruntled" employees were really feeling frustrated, overlooked, and unheard. By allowing them to tell their story and sharing with them my observations and understanding of their situation, we were able to come up with strategies to remotivate them, find ways for them to be successful, and help them begin to be recognized as a positive contributor. For some, this was a temporary fix, but for others, it resulted in a full turnaround in their careers. Their mojo returned, and their hallway reputation improved when people were confronted with the evidence before them of an engaged, motivated individual.

Asking about motivation is not only necessary for disgruntled employees. It is also important and useful for leading all your team members. I had another employee who told me he wanted to learn more about a particular area of operations. I found an upcoming project and made sure to put him on it. Not only did he perform well on this project, but because I had listened to him and worked to accommodate his interests, his overall attitude and work product on all his other tasks improved.

A third employee wanted difficult projects. The more complicated the better. He liked the challenge and the puzzle, and the sense of accomplishment in solving it himself. He did not want to be bothered with flattery; he just wanted the next challenge.

A fourth employee simply wanted to feel more like she was part of the team. She wanted to be invited to office lunches and activities when groups of us went out outside of work. We had not actively excluded her, but understanding how she felt about this and how it motivated her, we made sure to actively include her in future events.

Another thing to keep in mind is that motivation is dynamic. The conversation needs to be ongoing or at least needs to take place a couple of times a year. Okay, so I got the employee the award. What now? The glow of the award will last only so long. How can I keep him motivated? I got the other employee involved in the project he was interested in. What happens when the project is finished? If you approach motivation as a static concept that never changes, you will fail.

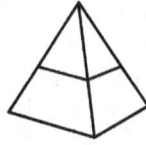

Here is the lesson:
You need to understand what motivates your individual team members and then take actions to implement those motivations. The motivations will be as varied as the employees themselves and the best way to discover motivation is to ask. Motivation is a dynamic concept, and you need to be constantly reevaluating what the current motivations are.

Note

1 The series *Severance* on Apple TV+ has an interesting take on separating work and personal life. In the show, employees voluntarily go through a medical procedure to sever their brains in such a way that when at work they remember nothing of their lives outside of work, and when outside of work, they remember nothing of their lives at work. The premise of the show, though, is that the characters at work feel incomplete and fight to know more about their nonwork selves.

REFERENCES

Everything DiSC. (2023). *What is the DiSC® model?* Wiley. www.everythingdisc.com/what-is-disc/

Goldberg, L. R. (1993). The structure of phenotypic personality traits. *American Psychologist, 48*(1), 26–34. https://doi.org/10.1037/0003-066X.48.1.26

Stitt, C. (2021, March). *Tell me your story: Recovering the unled and mismanaged.* WiLD Leaders. www.wildleaders.org/wild-articles/tell-me-your-story-recovering-the-unled-and-mismanaged

WiLD Leaders. (2025). *The WiLD Toolkit.* www.wildleaders.org/the-wild-toolkit

Chapter 9

Building alliances

If you want to lead the pack, you need to identify and deal with the alpha

Every group has a leader. In wolf packs, the leader is the alpha. This is the wolf that is the biggest and strongest, and the others are willing to follow. A similar pattern emerges in human interactions: for a variety of reasons, there is almost always one person who is the leader of a pack of people. This is true in both social settings and the business environment.

There is some great research on the concept of "tribal leadership" in human organizations by Dave Logan, John King, and Halee Fischer-Wright (Logan et al., 2008). In their book titled *Tribal Leadership: Leveraging Natural Groups to Build a Thriving Organization*, the authors explain how humans naturally form groups of 20 to 150 people, and how the whole group can be influenced by smaller groups of two to three people, which they refer to as dyads and triads. This structure strongly influences attempts at change management within the organization and the overall cohesiveness of the group. This research is key to understanding group dynamics and how to influence them.

When you show up in a new job and you are the "boss," you do not automatically become the leader. You may become the manager, but to become the leader is another level. Some work environments can be hostile to new managers. Maybe the people in the environment are entrenched in their methodologies and do not like change, or maybe their last manager did not gel with the group well. Maybe there are simply generational gaps between you and the employees. What you need to do, to make the shift from manager to leader, is overcome hostility or wariness. The best way to do this is to identify the current leader and get him or her on your side.

In some cases, identifying the alpha is easy. Everyone defers to them, and it is quickly apparent who is in charge. Your challenge, then, is to determine whether leaving that person as the alpha will aid in the accomplishment of your goals, and if not, what you will do with them.

John C. Maxwell has great insights into these types of situations in chapter 5 of his book *The 21 Irrefutable Laws of Leadership: Follow Them and People Will Follow You* (Maxwell, 1998). In this particular chapter,

DOI: 10.1201/9781003650454-12

Maxwell relates the story of arriving at his first church as a senior pastor, thinking that his title and position made him the leader. He discovered to his chagrin that this was not true. There was already an alpha in place. Maxwell describes how he learned to work with this person in a collaborative way to accomplish his goals, while ensuring respect for the alpha. This is like the challenge I faced in my Journeyman 1 assignment.

When I got to my assignment in Journeyman 1, I was moving into a brand-new position that had been created to oversee the section. The ambassador was very happy to have me, because he had been pushing for the creation of this position for a long time. Finally, it was filled. So, I had his support. The employees in the section, though, were a little wary, especially the guy who had been the de facto boss up until this point. Now, don't get me wrong. He was used to the fact that he had a regional supervisor who would pop in for a few days each quarter to see how things were going, but now I was on the ground in a permanent position, which knocked his prestige down a peg. This was especially true because this assignment was in a foreign county and in addition to personality issues, there were cultural dynamics at play.

He was not hostile to me, but he clearly wanted to assert himself. I don't blame him. He had been in his position for close to 20 years. On top of that, prior to joining my agency, he had been a high-ranking politician in his national government. So, he was used to being in charge and being deferred to.

When I came into the position, this alpha employee, now my second-in-command, treated me well, gave me a tour of the operation, and then introduced me to many of his local government contacts. It was clear he was in charge, and comfortable with it, but I immediately saw ways that I wanted to improve the program. One thing I needed was a little bit of time with him out of the way so I could get a real read on things. Sometimes fate intervenes.

As it turned out, the alpha was scheduled to travel to Washington, DC, for a week of training and was then planning to spend another week visiting friends there. I would get a chance to settle in, get a good look at the program, and start to form my own unfiltered opinions. Unfortunately, instead of spending the week in the office doing this, I came down with pneumonia, a really nasty case that almost landed me in the hospital. Well, I thought to myself as I returned to work a week later, I would at least have a couple of days before he was back.

It would be longer than that. As I settled in on Monday, I had no idea what a turn the world would take the next day. It was Monday, September 10, 2001. 9/11 was my third full day in the office.

As I mentioned in the preface, the pyramid I navigated through my career was the Department of State, and specifically the Bureau of Diplomatic Security. My assignment in Journeyman 1 was to a US Embassy in Africa. The events of 9/11 had a huge impact, especially for the new Regional

Security Officer on his third day in the office, especially as I was the first permanently assigned Regional Security Officer the embassy had ever had.

Coordinating the embassy's security response fell to me. I was 28 years old, had been in the office for three days, did not speak the local language very well (long story, for another book), had a small local guard force (no US Marine Security Guards, or MSGs, at this post at the time), and my second-in-command, the alpha, who had been running the program for 20 years and was personal friends with all of the major contacts, was in training in Washington, DC.

Luckily, I was well prepared from my previous assignment and the host government was very responsive, offering support and to shut down all the roads around the embassy. I gladly accepted. In all the chaos, shock, and fear of that day, we had no idea what to expect next.

The ambassador was very pleased with my reactions that day: every time he would think of things we could do to respond, I had already taken care of it: account for the staff, done; contact the host government, done (they had closed the streets around the embassy ten minutes earlier); reinforce the guard posts, in progress (we were calling in extra guards); set up a command post, next on my list. For me, I was just doing what I had been trained to do, although to the ambassador it looked like magic that I was able to stay ahead of the local developments. He ended up surprising me with a meritorious honor award at the end of the year (we'll discuss awards in a later chapter).

Another interesting development was that, with the alpha out of town, I was in direct control of the guard force, the surveillance detection team, and my other staff, and because of the events of that day and the following days, I was a whirlwind. By the end of the week, I was the alpha.

Because of the response to 9/11, my second-in-command was stuck in the US for a couple of weeks. This gave me time to cement my position as the alpha. As I examined my program, I really saw the strain that it was under, so I took steps to rectify that. I will go into this in more detail later in the book, but for the purposes of this chapter, it is important to understand that, as the new alpha, I did not just show my strength but also took steps to care for my pack.

When the previous alpha, now acknowledged by all as my second-in-command, finally returned, I was firmly in charge. This was a difficult thing for him. It had knocked his prestige and ego down several notches, and he was struggling with this. It would be difficult for anyone. We tried to work things out, but he was unhappy, and it showed, kind of like I would experience later in my mid-level 2 assignment as a deputy. Now there were several ways I could handle this: I could keep him in the pack, kill him (okay, we are not wolves, I would not kill him, but firing him would have the same effect), or he could go into exile and look for another pack to lead.

Keeping him in the pack, okay, office, would not have worked well. For one thing, I needed to set things up for my eventual replacement. Leaving my second-in-command in place would have potentially allowed him to take up his place as alpha again during the gap between my departure and my replacement's arrival. Second, he was unhappy, and it was affecting the morale of the rest of the office. Finally, I did not want him in a position to undo all the work I had been doing to professionalize and modernize the guard force by encouraging people to resist the changes and wait me out until I departed.

Firing him was also not a good option. He had put in close to 20 years of good service. He did his best with the resources available to him and had great contacts that were very helpful to us. Firing him would have been unfair to him, and the embassy.

So that left exile. For a while, the embassy had been looking to create a new position that would be a political-military specialist, but they were struggling with finding a suitable candidate. My second-in-command was a perfect fit, and he gladly jumped at the opportunity when he was offered it. He was back to being an alpha, though for a much smaller pack. He continued to do an excellent job and became a solid partner for me when I needed his experience, advice on the local situation, or help with a contact, or as we say in the Foreign Service, an interlocutor.

In the case I just laid out, identifying the alpha was easy, but that is not always the case. Sometimes there is a boisterous employee who distracts your attention, while the real alpha is quietly sitting in the background, monitoring events. This happened to me in the Journeyman 2 assignment.

When I rotated into Journeyman 2, my position was a newly created management position in an existing headquarters office. As with Journeyman 1, the office's basic structure and mandate had existed for a while, but I was being added as a new layer of management. Complicating this, my mandate was to "fix the program."

This is a broad mandate, but I was familiar with the program, as I had experience with it on the customer end overseas. One of the reasons I was in this new position was because I had spent the last four years offering suggestions on how to improve the program. It was really a case of leadership telling the hyper, young, wannabe, "well, if you know so much, then you fix it!" I was itching for this opportunity and challenge, but I knew I had to deliver, so there was some serious pressure.

Complicating this situation was that all my staff were retirees who had served full careers in the field, retired, and returned as part-time contractors. The one with the least experience in the office had been there for five years (after serving a full career in the field). I was 30 years old and had been with my agency for six years. But I was in charge, and I was going to lead these guys through a technological revolution: ah, youth and hubris!

For the most part, the retirees working for me were a great group of guys with a wealth of experience. For four out of five of them, they took their mandate as writ: this is our process and procedure we were told to follow; therefore, this is what we do. They were a solid, professional group, but because this was a part-time, post-retirement job, they were not looking to rock the boat, think outside the box, and invent new and different ways to do the job.

That said, these guys were pretty flexible and customer-service oriented. While they were not inclined to streamline the processes themselves, they were not particularly opposed to following new procedures and processes. So, while my leadership told to me to "fix the program," it quickly became apparent that my staff was not the problem, but rather the policies and procedures that had not been updated since 1994 did not move at the speed required for the post-9/11 world.

On arrival, I immediately keyed in on the fifth member of this group, who seemed to be the leader. He had set himself up to work more hours than the rest and had been involved in the successful implementation of the most recent changes. I figured that if I could get this guy on my side and following my path, the rest of the pack would fall into place. I could not have been more wrong.

As it turned out, the deal with this guy was that he was a self-promoter and, while he was very good at his job and had a wealth of experience, he was NOT the leader of this particular pack. In fact, he was very much an outsider, and the others had closed ranks against him. For the sake of argument, let's call him the "False Alpha." Luckily, I did not try to hitch my star to his wagon, because if I had, I would never have been successful in getting the rest of the pack to implement my ideas. One of the things I did with each of these guys was to spend some time with them: having coffee, dropping into their cubicles, engaging in casual conversations, and so forth.

Through this process, I began to realize that this guy was truly the False Alpha. He had some good ideas and put himself out front on a lot of issues, but the others did not follow him. They actually shunned him for his behavior.

So, this brought up the question: if I am going to be successful in leading these guys through my technological revolution, who do I REALLY need to get to buy into my plans? Who is the Real Alpha? As it turns out, it was the quietest of the bunch.

When I came into the office, I had four retirees working for me, and shortly after my arrival we added a fifth. For sake of this narrative, we had the False Alpha, the Real Alpha, and two acolytes, and a new initiate. While the False Alpha was busy promoting his ideas, the acolytes were busy promoting the status quo, and their frustration with the False Alpha was tangible. They were not following him, but clearly, neither of them was the real leader. The new initiate had just arrived, so he was not the alpha. This left the fifth individual, who quietly did his job, but I also noticed he was the one that both acolytes went to when they had questions, and the new initiate started doing so as well, and he was the one who calmed them when their frustrations ran highest. I had identified the Real Alpha. Now the trick was to ensure he would work with me, not against me.

As in the previous scenario, I had three choices: keep him in the pack, kill him, or send him into exile. I had these choices for both the False Alpha and the Real Alpha. In both cases, I chose to keep them in the pack.

Now, some may say that the easier solution may have been simply to get rid of them and send them into permanent retirement. However, the reality of the situation was that for budgetary reasons, to expand my team to give it the staffing needed, the easiest and most cost-effective way was to bring in a couple more part-time retirees. Additionally, as I have repeated, these guys were not the cause of the problem, and their experience gave them enormous credibility with the customers of the program around the globe.

If I had not been able to work around and through the False Alpha and through the Real Alpha, things might have turned out differently. As it was, once I recognized my initial misjudgment about the office power structure and took steps to correct it, things went pretty smoothly. However, there was one other wrinkle: I ended up having to convince the Real Alpha that he was, in fact, the de facto leader of the other employees.

The Real Alpha knew that the others (including the False Alpha) listened to him, but he had never actively wanted to become their leader. This had been a natural evolution over the several years that the group had worked together. Frankly, the Real Alpha had no intention of being the leader of the group; he wanted simply to do his job, follow the process and procedures, and enjoy his life outside of this part-time, post-retirement job.

As I started to finalize my master plan of how to "fix the program," I knew I needed to get the Real Alpha to buy into it. I knew that if I could get him to take this chance with me and support the changes, the others would follow suit. I also knew that I could not accomplish this without him: the acolytes were too committed to him, and removing him would have alienated them from me. So, I sat down with him and explained the situation.

As I said, at first, he was resistant: not to the changes, but to the idea that he held such sway in the office. As I laid out the situation, he began to understand that if he followed my lead, the two acolytes would follow him. This left the problem of the False Alpha. As is usually true with a False Alpha, the thing they dread most is being left behind, so when the rest of the pack made their turn to follow me, he followed them, solving that problem.

Leaving the Real Alpha as part of the pack had another benefit: as I have mentioned, he had been around for a while, and he was able to point out to me the difficulties I would have with some of my more outlandish suggestions. He also provided continuity as my successors rotated through the office. In my transition notes to my immediate successor and to the next one, I made sure to explain the true office power structure, identify the Real Alpha, and warn them about the False Alpha.

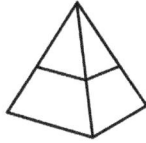

Here is the lesson:
You are not the leader just because your title says so. You need to identify and deal with the existing leader of the group before you can take charge. The real leader may not always be the one you first expect. Once you have identified the real leader, you have three choices: keep them and work with them, fire them outright, or send them into exile in another part of the organization. Many circumstances and variables will factor into determining the path that you choose.

REFERENCES

Logan, D., King, J., & Fischer-Wright, H. (2008). *Tribal leadership: Leveraging natural groups to build a thriving organization*. Harper Business.
Maxwell, J.C. (1998). *The 21 irrefutable laws of leadership*. Thomas Nelson.

Chapter 10

Discipline

Reprimand all to punish no one?

Everyone gets a medal, everyone gets an award, and everybody wins. Only each person loses. When there is a problem in the office, everyone gets reprimanded because we don't want to single anyone out. That is not leadership. That is not management. That is fear. That is a manager afraid to truly lead.

Many people are actually afraid to lead. It is a tremendous responsibility. Rob McKenna, CEO of Whole and Intentional Leader Development, regularly speaks about the paradoxes of leadership. One of these is the idea that when a person steps into a leadership role for the first time, or even when an experienced leader steps into a new role, there is a balance between readiness and wariness. He argues that the best leaders are the ones who understand the responsibility they are taking on, yet have the courage to do so.

Part of that responsibility involves enforcing discipline, having tough conversations with individuals. Because leading is all about working with people, and people are complicated, including the leaders themselves, there is a natural tension that arises when you are going into a conversation that may cause conflict between you and others. I have avoided conversations and mentally rehearsed them while envisioning the worst-case outcomes. What I have often found in reality is that when I have the conversation I need to have, it goes better than expected. I just needed to get up the courage to actually have the conversation.

Brené Brown, in her book *Dare to Lead: Brave Work. Tough Conversations. Whole Hearts*, writes about leaders who put on armor to protect themselves. In her surveys of senior leaders aimed at examining the skills that are needed today for tomorrow's leaders, one answer kept coming up, "We need braver leaders and more courageous cultures" (Brown, 2018). Brown emphasizes that fear—of failure, of vulnerability, or of criticism—often drives leaders to protect themselves rather than truly lead.

I attended a staff meeting during my mid-level 2 assignment at which my supervisor looked at everyone very gravely and excoriated us for behavior in which none of us engaged. The habit and culture of the group I worked

DOI: 10.1201/9781003650454-13

with was to arrive early, stay late, answer the phone after hours, provide great customer service, and complete our tasks on time or even ahead of time. Our supervisor, however, decided that he needed to have a stern talk with us about making sure we showed up on time and stayed until the end of the workday, that we made sure there was coverage in the office during the lunch hour, and so forth.

Throughout the day, after the meeting was over, each of my subordinates who were at the meeting came to me and asked, "what the hell was that about?" All I could do was shake my head and explain to them that the first time I heard about it was in the meeting as well. I also reassured them that I fully supported them, and they had individually done nothing wrong.

At the end of the day, I asked my supervisor about his comments and mentioned that all the staff were concerned. He responded by saying, "no, no one has done anything wrong, I just wanted to get it out there." What?!?!? Maybe, in making his comments to the staff, he was confused about who he should have been talking to. Let's just say, he did not exactly practice what he was preaching.

This was not the first time I experienced this. Everyone knows of a problematic employee, and everybody has probably experienced "the speech," where the supervisor says something like, "okay people, we have been getting a little lax on (fill in the blank: time sheets, coffee breaks, arrival time, departure time, lunch breaks, etc.) and we need to readjust. Therefore, from now on we are going to enforce the following rule." Rather than dealing directly with a problem employee, they paint the situation with a broad brush.

The thinking of the supervisor is that if they single someone out, they open themselves up to some sort of legal or personal liability. This causes them to be afraid. Therefore, instead of singling out the problem employee(s), they punish everyone, which only serves as a detriment to morale and a disruption to positive team dynamics. This can also lead to a decline in productivity. Luckily for my team, once I explained that no, our team had no issues, the boss was just ... who knows what, they were able to shake it off and continue on their way. The supervisor never brought up the topic again.

Leading an effective team requires trust. This trust can allow discretion and flexibility. Yes, the rules say that if you are going to be away from your desk for more than 15 minutes, you are required to have written permission from your supervisor, or you can be punished for being absent without leave. My agency even occasionally issued department-wide notices reminding employees of that rule. But what kind of work environment does that really foster? Is the work getting done? Is customer service being offered? Is anything falling through the cracks? If the answer is no, then where is the problem? By the way, can I point out that the computerized timekeeping system only works in one-hour increments, so trying to capture

15 minutes of missing time does not work anyway? More on that in the next chapter.

That said, there are employees who will take advantage of the system, who will abuse it, who will violate the trust of the team and disrupt the overall dynamic of high performance. Yes, I am singling you out. Because you abused the system and violated our trust. I am having a counseling session with YOU. Not the whole office or section. Because your actions have a negative impact on the workplace. Now, how are we going to address this? This also gives you the opportunity to find out if there are underlying issues the employee is facing that may need to be accommodated, or if this is truly a performance issue, and formal counseling and a performance improvement plan are warranted.

That is leadership. The employee is made aware that their behavior is unacceptable. The rest of the coworkers get the fact that the boss is trying to address the problem on an individual basis, not by blaming everyone. You do not need to publicize or broadcast that you are trying to take care of the problem on an individual basis. You do not need to make a big show of calling the person into your office. In fact, it is best if the problem is handled as discreetly as possible, but you should understand that word will get around. Either the problem employee themselves will let people know, or there will be a change in their behavior.

One advantage of bureaucracies is that they do have mechanisms for addressing problem employees. To use those mechanisms, there must be sufficient documentation to activate them. Unfortunately, many supervisors and managers believe the mechanisms for dealing with problematic employees are too cumbersome and time-consuming, so they fail to lead out of laziness. Some supervisors and managers shy away from conflict and choose not to document poor performance because they worry it will cause strain in the workplace, and they are afraid they will open themselves up to repercussions from the employees, so they fail to lead out of fear. One of the worst tendencies of a bureaucracy is the problematic employee who simply gets passed from one office to another, and managers never do anything about them.

If the problem warrants it, don't be afraid to follow your bureaucracy's procedures to document the issues and work with human resources (HR) to terminate the employee or, at the very least, ensure their annual review includes a review of the issues and steps taken to attempt to address it.

There are two schools of thought when someone gets fired: put heads on pikes or allow them to quietly slip away. In a bureaucracy, the second methodology is often followed. It again comes back to a concern over liability: by revealing why an employee was fired, do I open myself up to a lawsuit, even if the firing was justified? If the answer is even a vague "maybe," then the usual response is simply to let the fired employee slip quietly away and not make an example of them. This is why I was shocked, truly and utterly shocked, by an announcement made by my agency during the middle of my career.

There was an employee whose actions were so egregious that all employees in my agency were required to be informed that this particular employee had not just been terminated but also had been prosecuted and convicted for their behavior! As part of the sentencing, the judge wrote in language REQUIRING the agency to notify all employees of the circumstances and behavior that led to the firing and subsequent arrest and conviction. WOW! Talk about making an example out of someone! Not just fired, but arrested, prosecuted, and convicted. And like the town crier from days of yore, HR was required to spread the news and make everyone aware. Head on a pike.

I understand that there are some differences in this case, in contrast to one in which an employee is simply fired for nonperformance or even malfeasance. For one thing, because the employee was convicted, all the information surrounding the case becomes public record. There is no right to privacy claim there. Second, the actions in which the employee engaged, embezzling hundreds of thousands of dollars, were particularly egregious. On the other hand, this was the first time I had ever heard of a judge requiring an agency to inform all employees of the circumstances of the case.

This was not the only case of publicly airing the misdeeds of disciplined and terminated employees. There was a time in which, on a semiannual basis, HR released a department-wide notice of the number of employees who were given significant discipline (e.g., suspended without pay) or were terminated during the preceding period, and an overview of the reasons for the termination. No names, no details, but at least a reminder to employees and supervisors that the disciplinary process functioned and was available if needed and if the supervisor was willing to engage it.

Toward the end of my career, there was even a movement to punish supervisors who failed to take action with problematic employees. The department instituted a "failure to properly supervise" rule. Allowing problematic employees to disrupt the rest of the team through negligence, often caused by fear of reprisal or simply laziness, was itself determined to be worthy of discipline.

Speaking of fear of reprisal, one of the more interesting things I learned in my agency-mandated leadership training is the statistics on successful equal employment opportunity (EEO) complaints by employees who attempt to use an EEO complaint against their supervisor who disciplined them. The success rate of this type of retaliation is very low. "But," you say, "I believe that having an EEO complaint against me in my record will follow me for the rest of my career and impede my promotions." Statistically speaking, this is not true. Further, as far as your hallway reputation goes, being willing to stand up, take appropriate action, and resist in the face of reprisal will improve your standing as a leader and encourage your employees to follow both you and your example.

There is one activity that I thoroughly encourage, to protect you against reprisal and other liability: document everything. If you are having a problem with an employee, make sure you write a memo to file for each instance or set of instances. Make sure the counseling sessions are documented and signed by you and the employee. If the employee refuses to sign, document that on the form. If the employee is particularly contentious, have an appropriate witness, such as the second-line supervisor, or the employee advocate, present for the counseling session and make sure they sign the memorandum of counseling. Make sure to list how the employee can improve so you can show that you gave them a chance.

The truth is a counseling session only takes a few minutes. Having a simple verbal counseling session may be what it takes to get the employee to shape up. Give the employee defined goals of improved performance and a timeline to meet those goals. If this is just verbal counseling, make it a short timeline and let them know that failure to achieve the goals will result in written counseling. Don't be afraid to follow through. There is a difference between an employee who is having a difficult time (either in their life or in fitting into the office) and a truly problematic employee. If he or she is the former, he or she will either be able to fix the problem or recognize that the present situation is not working and move on to other opportunities. If he or she is the latter, that is, a problematic employee who truly desires to disrupt the workplace either out of ego or spite, then you need to contact your HR section early in the process and work with that office to ensure you are following all the proper procedures to have the employee relieved.

If you approach the situation in this way, you accomplish two things: 1) you give a weak employee or an employee in difficult circumstances a chance to rehabilitate themselves; 2) you authoritatively address truly problematic employees, which everyone else in the work unit will appreciate, increasing their trust in you and improving the team dynamics.

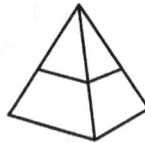

Here is the lesson:
Problematic employees exist. Deal with THEM. Trying to hide behind fears of liability or reprisal weakens you as a leader. Trying to spread the blame and judge everyone as guilty when they are not weakens you as a leader. Simply passing a problem employee off because you do not want to deal with them, turns you into a problem employee.

REFERENCE

Brown, B. (2018). *Dare to lead: Brave work. Tough conversations. Whole hearts.* Random House.

Chapter 11

Leadership character

When making rules, plan to enforce them

Following on the theme of discipline, it drives me a bit crazy when people make rules that they have no intention of enforcing. In my mind, if a rule is necessary, then you set it and enforce it. If not, then one of either two things happens: you did not need the rule in the first place, or you are setting yourself up for a failure of credibility. Credibility and integrity are two major components of leadership character, and if you lack those, good luck leading others.

Credibility and integrity are large and loaded terms. For the purposes of this chapter, I define credibility as someone who can be believed in and trusted. I define integrity as being consistent in word and deed, being honest, and being of sound moral principles.

There has been a lot written about the importance of credibility as foundational to leadership. Two authors who study this extensively are James Kouzes and Barry Posner. In the seventh edition of their book *The Leadership Challenge, How to Make Extraordinary Things Happen in Organizations*, they explain, "Leaders must be diligent in always guarding their credibility. The ability to take strong stands, challenge the status quo, and move in new directions depends on being highly credible. You can't take your credibility for granted" (Kouzes and Posner, 2023, p. 24).

Integrity is also essential to leadership. Being inconsistent between what you say and what you do, cutting corners, favoring some people and not others, failing to follow through on your commitments, and violating ethical principles all can undermine your integrity.

So, let's explore how this applies to rulemaking and enforcement in the workplace. Let's focus on making enforceable rules (credibility) and choosing when and how to enforce them when leading others (integrity).

There are two sorts of rules in the workplace: official, agency-wide rules, and local manager-made rules. The working theory is kind of like federal law versus state law and local laws, which can be made stricter than federal but cannot be made to circumvent federal laws. Another way of thinking of this is that the agency-wide rules are the laws, and the manager-made

DOI: 10.1201/9781003650454-14

rules are the implementing guidance. Sometimes, you will also encounter manager-made "rules" that are not really enforceable unless they have some basis in the overarching policies of the organization.

I had a manager once who firmly believed in a literal interpretation of the agency rules, even when the agency rules made little sense in our work environment. As I mentioned in the last chapter, my agency came out with an edict that "if you are away from your desk for more than 15 minutes without written permission from your supervisor, you are liable to be reprimanded as absent without leave." Really? Fifteen minutes? But my supervisor held a staff meeting and made sure we all understood this and that our time sheets were to be kept in 15-minute increments. Okay, several problems with this: 1) the rule did not say to keep the time sheet in 15-minute increments; 2) the computerized timekeeping system only lets you enter in blocks of an hour, so by keeping your time in 15-minute increments, all you are doing is driving the timekeeper insane; 3) the kind of workplace we worked in had us running to meetings all the time, sometimes on short notice, so if I disappeared for an hour without telling my supervisor, who himself was not sitting at his desk because he was at a meeting, was I liable? No one ever really came up with an answer to that one. Unfortunately, this inability to explain and interpret this rule for our work environment, coupled with the insistence that it be followed to the letter, undermined this supervisor's credibility.

Now this begs the question: why come out with such a rule in the first place? Is there such a horrendous propensity for employees to slough off their work that you really need to make such a rule? Are you trying to look tough because someone in Congress (probably a staffer and not even a member) asked a question about employee work habits? Are you trying to justify the need for more employees, and do you need some metrics about how much can be accomplished if employees are chained to their desks?

Honestly, there are a lot of potential good reasons to have such a rule for certain worksites and job descriptions, but to impose it agency-wide is an unfortunate side effect of the fear of singling out classes of employees. So, the knee-jerk reaction is to create a rule and attempt to apply it on a "fair and consistent basis" against all employees of the agency, even if it does not make sense for large swaths of the agency. This is not leadership: this is fear. Fear of lawsuits and grievances.

This problem is further compounded by supervisors who take this literal view of the rules and attempt to put a square peg in a round hole. The point is, the rule doesn't fit the work environment, but rather than attempt to make sensible, credible rules that fit the work environment, the supervisor attempts to wedge the work environment within the confines of the rule. Again, this is not leadership; this is fear. In this case, the supervisor is afraid of being seen as not being proactive and not toeing the line of upper management. The supervisor wants to be seen as rushing to the line to be first, hoping upper management will see what a good supervisor he is at implementing their directives, rather than questioning those directives. What do you see as the consequences of acting this way? Does this increase the supervisor's credibility with the team? Does it reflect integrity? Does it show leadership?

If the rules do not make sense, then as a leader, it is your job to question them and work to get them changed. Doing this shows integrity because you have questioned the underlying premise of a rule that does not make sense rather than either applying it unevenly or not at all. It also increases your credibility because you are taking steps to improve the working conditions for your team while seeking clarity of the requirements. I have actually had a lot of success in getting rules and policies changed, on an agency-wide basis, because I questioned the logic. I will discuss this more in Part 3: Leading Organizations.

In my agency I saw this time and again. It is one thing to examine the infraction of a rule and determine, based on the totality of the circumstances, that the infraction did not merit a reprimand or other discipline. In fact, giving honest consideration to the circumstances enhances both your credibility and your integrity. It goes the other way too: you may examine the circumstances and determine that discipline is required. In that case, it is important to follow through and dole out that discipline.

Some newer leaders may be hesitant to do so because they want to be liked. What these leaders do not realize, however, is that failing to follow through undermines their credibility and integrity, not just in the eyes of the person meriting discipline, but the whole team.

Brené Brown has a lot to say about this in her book *Dare to Lead*, mentioned earlier. One of her mantras is "Clear is kind, Unclear is unkind" (Brown, 2018). She shows that choosing to be liked rather than choosing to have necessary tough conversations is a leadership failure. Courageous leaders value clarity, accountability, and respect, not just approval.

Effective leadership requires prioritizing courage over personal comfort. Leaders who seek to be liked rather than respected often shy away from accountability, weakening trust and performance within their teams. By choosing courage over comfort, leaders model integrity and foster healthier, more resilient organizations (Brown, 2018).

As I explained earlier, there are various levels of rules, the ones that come from above and affect the whole pyramid, and the ones that you as the supervisor and leader create for your own little sub-pyramid. How much sense does it make to simply ignore the existence of the rule that you yourself created or signed off on? Doing this quickly undermines both your credibility and integrity. Credibility and integrity are hard to build but easy to shatter.

My supervisor in my mid-level 2 assignment took this one step further. He created a policy that he specifically had no intention of ever enforcing just so he could show headquarters that he had the policy in place. Talk about a lack of integrity. Sadly, when headquarters asked about the enforcement of the policy, my supervisor explained that while he had the policy in place, he felt no need to enforce it, and the inspectors from headquarters simply shrugged and said, "well, at least you have the policy in writing." So, in addition to the supervisor showing a lack of integrity by creating a policy he had no intention of enforcing, the headquarters personnel reviewing the situation showed a lack of credibility by accepting the situation. Is it any wonder why people have issues trusting bureaucracies?

Earlier, I wrote about agency-wide policies that do not fit all worksites or categories of employees. My agency does at least recognize this possibility and generally gives a certain amount of flexibility to local heads of the worksites. On certain policies, my agency gives broad guidelines that can be more tightly focused based on local circumstances, but for other policies, especially those involving life safety issues, there are firmer boundaries.

In response to an incident in which an employee was killed in the line of duty several years ago, my agency decided that advisories and recommendations about how to behave in overseas environments were not strong enough. Certain local policies were now required to be issued as "directives" by the person at the top of the local pyramid, typically the ambassador. Further, the penalties for failing to follow these policies are required to be spelled out, along with the mechanisms for requesting exceptions to these policies.

When I got to my mid-level 2 assignment, I noticed that this change had not yet been implemented at my worksite, so I started to examine the existing policies, redraft them in the new format, and push them up the local pyramid for approval. The first policy directive I drafted was simple and introduced this new system, explaining the purpose of the new style of policies. This document presented the background on why these directives were being issued, the consequences for violating the directives (e.g., counseling, suspension, removal from the embassy or termination of employment, depending on the severity of the infraction), and the process for seeking an exemption from the policy on a one-time or consistent basis. This introductory directive was approved without issue.

The second one ran into trouble in the approval process: the top of the local pyramid struck all the language about enforceability. The reason for this was not simply because including the disciplinary language in each one was repetitive and added unnecessary length (we tried that argument, but headquarters pushed back and insisted the disciplinary language was included in each directive), but rather was simply that the person at the top of the pyramid and his deputy did not want such strict language in the policy. They did not have issues with the overall content of the policy. It had been tailored to be appropriate for our local operating environment. They simply did not want any of the language regarding enforcement, consequences, or exceptions included.

It is important to note that the reason exceptions needed to be documented and approved was because these were life safety issues. Remember, the whole origin of this process was because an employee had been killed in the line of duty after deciding that complying with the existing embassy security policies was too burdensome.

My supervisor decided again that it was better to have a policy that was unenforceable rather than have no policy at all and simply folded. After that, we issued about a dozen of these kinds of policies; more than two-thirds of my drafts were rewritten to be unenforceable. Fortunately, the headquarters offices started to look at these directives more carefully, and during an assessment of our program, forced the redevelopment of these directives to include the required language on consequences and exceptions. The headquarters personnel rebuilt some of their credibility in the eyes of our team with that.

Now, in contrast, toward the end of this particular tour of duty, my agency conducted a survey to determine an appropriate cost-of-living allowance for our location. Whereas the top of the local pyramid had struck the language about enforcing life safety policies we issued, when it came to this survey, he sent out a strongly worded statement to all employees that if they failed to complete the survey, they would be reprimanded for failure to follow management instructions and that this failure would be required to be documented in the offender's annual performance review. The result of such documentation would have an impact on the offender's promotion potential not just that year, but since the last five years of performance reviews are considered by promotion panels, it would effectively shelve the employee for several years. Talk about lacking credibility and integrity: participation in a survey that could lead to an increase in pay was more of a priority than ensuring life safety.

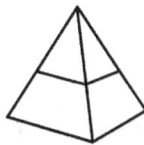

Here is the lesson:
Credibility and integrity are critical components of leadership character. Both are hard to build and easy to shatter. One of the clearest views into a leader's credibility and integrity is how they enforce rules, especially the ones they have promulgated themselves.

REFERENCES

Brown, B. (2018). *Dare to lead: Brave work. Tough conversations. Whole hearts.* Random House.

Kouzes, J. M., & Posner, B. Z. (2023). *The leadership challenge* (7th ed.). Wiley.

Chapter 12

Developing others

Be a good Dungeon Master

When I was in middle school, I was introduced to *Dungeons & Dragons*.[1] I played a bit here and there, particularly with my friends Josh and Mike, whom I mentioned in Chapter 1. After high school, I did not play again for years. For whatever reason, though, I hung on to my dice and a few other accoutrements. I always rather enjoyed the role-playing and fantasy aspects of the game: magical powers and implements, superhuman abilities, and the concept of gaining experience points to advance in levels. I was never very serious or fanatical about the game, but I enjoyed it just the same.

One day, 20 years after high school, a colleague of mine approached me at an office happy hour and asked if I, by chance, might enjoy a roll of the dice as he was putting together a group for some adventuring. I bit, and I am glad that I did. In addition to being able to reengage with some fond memories of my youth, the group that my Dungeon Master put together was a fun bunch.

Also, it was an interesting contrast playing later in life, with the job and life experience I had, playing with a group of super-intelligent folks with a mind for role-playing. As a group, we kicked butt. As I played, though, and had a more mature understanding, I began to realize how important it is to have a good Dungeon Master and the parallels that can be drawn to leadership in a bureaucracy.

In *Dungeons & Dragons*, the characters are established on paper, and you roll dice to determine various scores on a range of criteria: strength, agility, intelligence, wisdom, constitution, and charisma. The concept is that by rolling dice, the baselines are established, just as fate and genetics establish these factors in real people. These are the baselines, the strengths and weaknesses of the individual character. You also typically come up with a backstory for your character, a brief historical sketch of who your character is and how they have come to abandon their homes and normal lives to go off in search of adventure.

The player is then responsible for making the most of the character's strengths while minimizing the impact of the weaknesses, to complete the

DOI: 10.1201/9781003650454-15

series of tasks that the Dungeon Master sets out. The role of the Dungeon Master is to create a program of activities (such as a one-off quest or a continuing adventure campaign) that allow the characters to gain experience, learn new skills, and accomplish the goal of the adventure ... or die trying.

Now, in case you have not yet made the quantum leap of imagination, let me draw a couple of parallels for you: the characters, role-played by the players, are the employees. The Dungeon Master is the supervisor/manager/leader. All characters start out as level one. They are fragile: they do not have many hit points (the number of blows they can take before they die), and they are not advanced in their skills and abilities. For instance, a magic user does not have a wide variety of spells to choose from, and a thief is not as good at opening locks or looking for traps.[2] A good Dungeon Master understands this and will select adventures that allow the characters to gain experience but won't get them killed within the first couple of encounters.

It might be possible that if the player makes a serious error in judgment, their character could be seriously hurt or killed, in which case the player has the option of making a new character and starting over from Level 1 or leaving the game in disgrace. As the game progresses, the character gains more abilities, and as the player becomes more skilled, the challenges increase as well. (Okay, are you keeping up, or do I really need to draw the parallel here between Level 1 characters and entry-level employees?)

Adventures are rarely solo. Typically, you have a "party," a team of adventurers of different skill sets that work together to unravel the mysteries of the game module they are playing (in real life, we call this the work team, office, focus group, etc.). The Dungeon Master has selected the module based on their understanding of the level of the characters combined with the skill of the players.

The Dungeon Master wants to run a module that is challenging and fun, offering opportunities for advancement while keeping the players engaged and entertained. If the module is too hard, the game will be over quickly, and the players will be frustrated. If the module is too easy, the game will be over quickly, and the players will be bored and complacent. Sometimes, if a new player joins the group, the Dungeon Master may pull back and go to a slightly easier module to see how well the new player fits in with the group, without disrupting the overall level of the game.

Many of the adventures are mysteries: there is some sort of puzzle that needs to be identified and then solved. Sometimes, the Dungeon Master will clearly explain the goal of the overall module to the party. Other times, the Dungeon Master will give clues about the mystery to one or more of the players to see how those players handle the information and share it with the rest of the group. A good Dungeon Master makes sure that the party stays on track and does not get overly distracted from the main purpose by the individual encounters.

Some Dungeon Masters will attempt to follow a very strict script as to how the adventure will unfold. A good Dungeon Master will follow the outlines of a module, suggesting or hinting at how a problem should be handled if the group does not answer it in a way that fits the outline. A GREAT Dungeon Master will allow the party the freedom to creatively address the problems, even if the solutions are surprising. Some of the best evenings my group has had in adventuring have included "Aha, WOW" moments in which one of the players took an action that was completely in character but that was unexpected by the Dungeon Master, who has been flexible enough to recognize the utility of the solution and incorporate it into the game.

As the game continues, the players become more comfortable with their roles, and the players and Dungeon Master begin to anticipate how they will react to different scenarios. This familiarity allows the problem-solving to move more quickly as the group understands to staff out different challenges to various characters who are better suited to them. The challenge for the Dungeon Master is then to mix things up enough to allow for continued player/character development and to keep things from getting stagnant. This may involve sending a character off on an individual quest, adding a new player to the group, or picking a module that is very different from what the group has typically played.

As the group tackles each module and successfully completes it, there is only one thing left to do at the end: divide up the treasure and determine which players have gained enough experience points to be promoted to the next level. After all, one of the goals of a good Dungeon Master is to get the characters promoted at a pace on par with the development of the player. If a character is promoted too quickly, the player will not have the experience to understand how best to interact at the higher levels. If a character is promoted too slowly, the player will become frustrated and may simply leave the game.

In real life, the character and the player are one in the same: the employee. Genetics and fate have issued us different scores or levels for our personal traits (strength, intelligence, wisdom, charisma, etc.), though instead of listing them on paper for people to read, we have the hallway reputation where that information is passed around. We write out our histories in the form of curricula vitae or résumés and one-page bio statements.

The office manager/team leader is the Dungeon Master, selecting the challenges that the team or the office of employees will address. A good leader will ensure that the projects issued out will aid in the development of the employees, helping them learn new skills and abilities and giving each of them a chance to take on a leadership role themselves. Once a team is established, a great leader will give that team flexibility in addressing the challenges, even if the answers are surprising. In the case of a surprising or really "outside the box" answer, a great leader will consider whether the answer is acceptable and workable in the overall context of the job, rather than simply dismissing it out of hand.

A good leader will ensure that the group stays on track with their assignments and deadlines, rather than being led astray by interesting, though less important, side projects. I am not saying that side projects are not useful, particularly if they can be wrapped back into the overall goals of the office, but the main purpose of the office still needs to be accomplished. Allowing the pursuit of side projects or interests may have substantial benefits to the main purpose or goal. For instance, I learned a lot about SharePoint by working on side projects for other offices, which I have been able to bring back to increase the effectiveness and efficiency of my own office. At the same time, if you get too far off your main tasks, you may start to miss deadlines and/or experience other detrimental effects to your principal purpose.

When I was in entry-level 2, I had a supervisor like this, and it is the reason I was ready to take on the challenges of Journeyman 1 and beyond. As someone once phrased it, my supervisor was "very good at giving you enough rope to hang yourself but would step in to prevent you from tying the knot." My supervisor gave me a certain level of freedom to do the job, but she also paid attention to making sure that I, and the others in the office, did not get too far off track. She was also very good at sharing her experience to aid in our development. For instance, when I would write a report on an incident, she would show me how subtle changes in the phrasing could have a huge impact on how it was received by headquarters, both to get them to pay attention when we needed it and to soothe their concerns if it was a particularly sensitive topic.

There was one instance when we had an employee with a serious conduct violation that required a decision from upper management on how they wanted to address it (local discipline or removal from the embassy). This was a pressing, time-sensitive issue, but my supervisor took the time to lay out options for us to address the issue and her recommendation, just as she was about to do for upper management. In this case, she accomplished two goals: 1) she dealt effectively with the problem employee, and 2) she mentored us and showed us how we could deal with and communicate similar situations in the future. This is an example of excellent leadership: showing us how to navigate the dungeon, or in real life, the pyramid of the bureaucracy. She was, in effect, a more experienced Dungeon Master helping her people navigate a potentially challenging play.

During another stage of my career, I was back at headquarters in Washington. I was working on a project that would transform how the entire department would accomplish one of its major global tasks (in Part III, I'll discuss key concepts related to leading organizations, regardless of your position in the pyramid, and go into more detail about this project).

I came up with a briefing about how I planned to accomplish the goals. I gave the briefing to my division chief, and instead of saying, "Okay, I'll run it up the chain," he said, "Okay, let's run it up the chain." He then accompanied me as we went to his boss, the office director. When the office director asked me if I could really accomplish what I was proposing, my division chief piped up and said he had full faith and confidence in my ability to do this, and he would ensure I had the resources I needed to get it done. What a great Dungeon Master! (or maybe pyramid master?)

"Okay," the office director said, and then facilitated a meeting for us with the deputy assistant secretary. He liked the idea, so they took me to the principal deputy assistant secretary. The PDAS liked my idea as well but recognized my briefing was too long for more senior levels. For the Assistant Secretary, instead of 30 minutes to present my proposal, I would have seven, plus three minutes for questions (I'll discuss more about communicating up the pyramid in the next chapter).

The division chief, office director, and Deputy Assistant Secretary helped me streamline the presentation to be most effective. They also made sure I got on the schedule with the Assistant Secretary. The Assistant Secretary was so impressed with my briefing that he said, "This is great, this is exactly what we need. Your presentation is solid. I have a meeting with all the other Assistant Secretaries in ten minutes. Can you give this presentation again at that meeting?" WOW! And then, instead of the Assistant Secretary giving my brief for me, he introduced me and let me give it.

This is leadership on several levels:

- Giving credit where it is due
- Helping to improve the presentation
- Supporting the project and following through.

At every level, my supervisor and the supervisors above him helped me navigate the Dungeon (okay, pyramid), map the way, avoid the traps, and stand my ground in the face of adversity. All of this resulted in a very successful quest!

Here is the lesson:

One of your principal jobs in leading others is to ensure their development: giving them appropriate tasks for their skill level, building trust in themselves and their abilities, and giving them challenges to stretch and grow. The best leaders provide appropriate directions or reorientation when needed to ensure things stay on track, but also allow the employees the opportunity to find creative ways to solve problems. Share experience and wisdom. Help them learn how to navigate the pyramid so they are ready to move to the upper levels.

Notes

1   According to Britannica, *Dungeons & Dragons* (D&D) is "a fantasy role-playing game (RPG), created by American game designers Ernest Gary Gygax and David Arneson in 1974 and published that year by Gygax's company, Tactical Studies Rules (TSR). The game was acquired in 1997 by Wizards of the Coast, a subsidiary of Hasbro, Inc." Source: Britannica. (n.d.). Dungeons & Dragons. In *Britannica*. www.britannica.com/topic/Dungeons-and-Dragons

2   As an aside, I always found it more interesting to play a dual-class character; in *D&D* I played a fighter/cleric, strong and good with weapons, but with a spiritual side that allowed him to tap into mysticism and magic. In real life, I play a knight-in-bodyarmor/policy-process-technology wizard.

Chapter 13

How to use awards

"You like me, you really really like me!"

Many of you will have heard the story of Sally Field accepting an Academy Award for Best Actress and saying her famous lines in 1985. The title of this chapter is the commonly accepted misquote. Ms. Field, upon winning the Academy of Motion Pictures award for Best Actress for *Places in the Heart*, actually said, "I haven't had an orthodox career, and I've wanted more than anything to have your respect. The first time I didn't feel it, but this time I feel it, and I can't deny the fact that you like me, right now, you like me!" (Waxman, 1999).

Is the misquote important? Probably not, though I find it amusing, and it also says something about the misunderstanding people have about awards themselves and how they come about. Awards can be a powerful tool. They can motivate and reward employee actions. They can show respect to your team members and demonstrate good leadership. But not all awards are created (or rather bestowed) equally.

Some people think they deserve an award and lobby hard for it, even if the actions they took are a basic part of their job requirements. Some people routinely go above and beyond their job requirements because that is their nature and character, and they never request or expect an award for it. They may even be embarrassed when they receive one.

In my view, there are five kinds of awards you can receive. The amount of effort that you personally put into the nomination process is inversely proportional to the amount of respect the award engenders. The continuum goes like this:

1) Awards you give yourself.
2) Awards you suggest that:
    a) You provide support for, and
    b) Someone else writes for you.
3) Awards you write yourself.
4) Awards you support.
5) Awards that show you are truly respected.

DOI: 10.1201/9781003650454-16

Awards you give yourself are just that. Yes, someone else may be listed as the nominator, but in reality, you suggest the award to the nominator and fully write the justification, and even the citation. Hey, no question, you may have deserved that award. You may have worked your butt off and accomplished something that no one else ever has, and the reason you had to write the award that you fully deserve is that the supervisor you work under failed to recognize your accomplishment without some major prompting: shame on them. Or, you might simply be a self-promoter who thinks you deserve an award for passing air in and out of your chest for seven hours and 15 minutes a day (of course, you take the full 45 minutes for lunch; you are entitled to it, right?), and you managed to bamboozle your boss into signing the form you stuck in front of them. In which case, shame on you.

Almost as sad are the awards that you suggest. If you need to point out to management that you deserve an award, it is only slightly better than writing the entire thing yourself. This at least breaks into two levels of respect: management agrees and asks you to provide input so they can write the award, or management agrees and undertakes the writing and nomination process themselves. In the first case (2a), it is almost as bad as giving yourself the award, but at least in this case management fully agrees that your performance is deserving of an award. They are just not familiar enough with what you actually did, so they ask you to provide some bullet points or text that they can and do modify. By taking ownership of the award process, they are at least recognizing that you are worthy of the award, and are putting forth some effort to help you get it. Unfortunately, in my estimation, 2a is probably the most common kind of award in a bureaucracy.

The second category (2b) of awards you suggest is one in which you point out that your work is worthy of an award, and the management agrees and is clued in enough to what you did to actually write it themselves. In this case, you start with a lazy supervisor, but at least they perk up when you poke them. They may have taken some prompting, but once engaged, they show some leadership in the process. They might ask for some clarification, but they have taken ownership of the process, and they will work to get you the award that you rightly deserve.

Now we move down on the list to level 3, and up on the spectrum of respect to awards that the supervisors themselves recognize you deserve, but being too busy, lazy, or for whatever other reason, they ask you to write up the nomination yourself. They have recognized the excellent effort you put forth, which shows you respect and makes you feel good, so you are probably more than happy to write the whole thing up for them, ready for their signature. If you are lucky, once you provide them with the initial write-up, they will add to it, strengthen it, and take back some of the ownership for the process.

The second-to-last level on the continuum (level 4) are awards when the supervisor recognizes you deserve an award and they have a good idea of how it should be written, but they ask you for some support, bullet points, proofreading, and so forth to make sure they got the details right. The supervisor has almost complete ownership of the process. They recognized your accomplishment as worthy of an award and had enough knowledge of what you did to basically write it themselves, but they are showing you respect by making sure that they fully capture the accomplishment. You can be proud of these kinds of awards; they are almost as good as the final level. In my estimation, this (level 4) is probably the second-most common kind of award.

Awards that truly show respect for you come as a surprise (level 5). The first indication that you have been nominated for an award is when you receive an invitation to the awards ceremony, or, in my estimation just as good, is when you are presented with a completed, signed nomination and told that it has been submitted for consideration. I would even put awards that you do not receive, but are nominated for in this way, into this category. In this case, management is fully engaged, they are paying attention, and they appreciate your efforts. This shows outstanding leadership and deepens the mutual respect between the leader and the led.

Think for a minute: what kind of award would you most like to receive? As I said earlier, in my view, the amount of effort you yourself put into the award is inversely proportional to the amount of respect you feel when you receive it.

In a perfect world, all the awards would be level 5. But we do not live in a perfect world, so as I mentioned, in my estimation the most common kind of award is level 2, with level 4 coming after that. In fact, I would say that level 5 awards are probably the rarest.

In the first half of my career (the part this book is focused on), I received two level 5 awards. Interestingly, the first one of these was a significant award with a nice monetary bonus attached to it, presented at a work-site wide awards ceremony. I had nominated several of my employees for awards, and when I received the invitation to the awards ceremony, I simply assumed that it was so I would be there to see them receive their recognition. I was shocked, and a little confused, when my name was called and I was asked to come forward so the ambassador could present me with a meritorious honor award for my efforts surrounding the embassy response to 9/11.

The second was a simple ginned-up certificate of appreciation that I received in the mail one day. I had worked on a project for another office, making sure to follow their guidance and report back on the results. For me, it felt kind of standard and routine. But for the other office I had assisted, they truly appreciated how thorough I had been and how easy I was to work with. That little certificate stands proudly in the portfolio containing all my other awards.

My appreciation for both of these awards was the same. While I was toiling away, doing my job and accomplishing my tasks, someone had taken notice and taken their own time and effort to ensure my accomplishments were recognized. I felt an incredible level of respect both for the awards and from the people who had taken the time to ensure I was recognized. This effort shows tremendous leadership credibility and integrity. It also increased my motivation to continue focusing on delivering high-quality work.

Recent research affirms that my sense of appreciation for both awards, one monetary and the other a simple certificate of appreciation, is common. Shibeal O'Flaherty, Michael T. Sanders, and Ashley Whillans conducted a series of studies in 2021 that "examin[ed] the impact of light-touch, cost-effective interventions designed to promote the overall happiness of social workers" (O'Flaherty et al., 2021). They examined the impact of "Symbolic awards," which they categorized as "congratulatory cards, public recognition, and certificates" to increase motivation and performance, even if there was no monetary component. They found that the employees who received these kinds of noncash recognition felt significantly more valued, more recognized for their work, and more supported by their organization than did those who did not receive this kind of recognition.

This may also explain why I was so touched and held on to letters and notes of appreciation throughout my career. It also has interesting implications for the effect of The Kindness Games movement I discussed in Chapter 2. But I digress… This chapter is really about utilizing the tools of your organization's formal awards process.

When I write award nominations, I try to stick to level 5 awards. This takes a lot of effort because you really need to pay attention to what is going on with your team. Sometimes, merely because of the pace of events and the number of people moving in different directions at once, I slip into level 4 awards. Even here, though, the idea of the award was mine because I was in sync enough with my team to recognize that they merited an award.

I have never signed an award for levels 3, 2, or 1. Interestingly, on a couple of occasions (three, so far as I recall), one or another of my employees had come to me and suggested that their work or the work of a colleague was worthy of an award. In all three cases I had to confess that either I had already submitted the nomination or was already in the process of writing it.

In no way, shape, or form do I advocate giving out unmerited awards. If the work does not deserve an award, I will not be the nominator. Again, it is a matter of credibility and integrity. I believe it is important to show respect for the individual employee, the whole team, the awards process, and myself as a leader. Passing out undeserved awards cheapens the process. This again comes down to being in sync with your team, which starts with appropriate development of work requirements, coupled with direction and oversight for completion of those work requirements.

When you decide that an action is deserving of an award, you need to then decide what kind. Most organizations have scaled levels of awards. One of the biggest problems in a bureaucracy is award inflation. Yes, the employee deserves an award for their action or accomplishment, but there is often a tendency to go for the highest-level award with the greatest amount of cash. This also undermines the awards process and the significance of awards.

My agency has tried to combat this by developing strict guidelines on what sort of action or accomplishment merits the different levels of awards. Even within award levels, there are scaled levels of monetary remuneration. An independent awards committee instructed to watch for inflation and undeserved awards is also part of the process. These factors help the awards process retain a semblance of credibility, but credibility truly starts with the nominator.

One of the harder things for me is giving different levels of awards to different employees, at the same time. There is a danger that an employee who receives a lower-level award will be offended and accuse you of playing favorites. This is another reason why you need to be sure that each employee merits his or her award and that the level of the award is justified.

Even employees who are generally seen as problem employees can do something that merits an award. I have found that giving a problem employee an award is often the key to starting to bring them around, especially if the underlying problem is that they are frustrated by a lack of recognition, which causes them to be disgruntled. I have used this technique several times, and it works for several reasons: it lets the employee know you truly appreciate their work (if not their attitude), and it gives them a sense of pride and accomplishment. For this technique to be effective, though, the same rules apply: the award must be merited based on performance or accomplishment, and the justification for the level of the award must be documented.

As I said, in my assignment to mid-level 1, I had two employees with serious attitude problems. One had felt like they had simply been run over and left behind by the organization. They were a pretty good employee, but their personality did not mesh particularly well with the rest of the office, so many people wrote them off. They came to me early in my tenure in the office and asked if I would write them up for an award. I deferred; I told them it was too early for me to do it, but we also laid out a plan, some milestones that they could achieve that would allow me to justify it. Over the next several months, as they hit the milestones and had accomplishments I could document, the award nomination basically wrote itself. Getting the nomination through the supervisors was also eased because the supervisors had seen the change in the employee and recognized the list of accomplishments that added up to the nomination. When they received the award, the employee became one of my strongest assets. I was the third or fourth supervisor who had promised them an award, but I was the first to lay out an action plan and follow through with it.

The other problem employee in this assignment remained a problem employee. They had a minor attitude adjustment that lasted a couple of weeks but then fell back into their old patterns. They deserved the award, but I think that part of the temporary adjustment was that they had an accomplishment that merited the award, and it was a substantial award, but it was a one-time accomplishment rather than something they had built up to. There is a lot of research going back decades on the reasons behind how monetary awards may lead to a temporary boost in productivity, but without sustained recognition or other nonmonetary incentives (such as personal development opportunities, a positive work environment, and an on-going recognition program), the boost quickly fades and employees fall back into their old patterns. Daniel Pink's book *Drive* takes a deep dive into these concepts (Pink, 2009).

Some supervisors have a habit, in an effort to ensure there is a perception of equity and parity in the office, to simply put everyone in for a group award. I think this is a cop-out. Yes, I have nominated a group for an award, but it was because the task they engaged in was a team effort. Typically, I try to individualize the awards as much as possible. This starts with developing the work requirements.

Take, for example, a presidential visit that we hosted during one of my overseas assignments: everyone in my office had basically the same job to do. The difference was that we divvied up the tasks appropriately. In reality, we did this for operational reasons to ensure all of the bases were covered for the different sites and moving parts of the visit. When it came time to write the awards (and later the employee evaluations), because we had differentiated the tasks, I was easily able to put the members of my team in for individual awards rather than a single group award.

Now, for the visit, I did put one team in for a group award. I did this because the task they worked on was a true group effort, executed as a seamless team. They all worked equally hard on the project, and to single out one of them above the rest would have done a disservice to the team. Another factor was that this was a small work team, five people. It made sense to put them in for a group award, so that is how I nominated them.

Contrast this to a couple of group awards I have received: a group award for everyone who showed up for a large conference (60 people, on one group award), a group award for everyone who helped with an Independence Day reception (80 people, on one group award), and a group award for everyone who helped with the visit of a VIP (the same 80 people, on one group award). Did I do something extraordinary to merit the award, other than show up at the right place at the right time? No, I did my job, and so did most of the other people on the award nomination, some with more passion, some with less.

What about those people who did something truly excellent, really meriting an award? You can only get one award and are part of the group. Imagine how frustrating that can be: you put in 110% and really do an excellent job, only to be lumped into a group award that literally everyone who happened to be in the general area got, regardless of the effort they truly put in. The larger the group, the more varied the levels of effort. One way to handle this MIGHT be to carve the large groups into smaller groups, which requires some effort to differentiate the tasks.

The one advantage of the large group award is how it is reflected in our employee profiles, which are reviewed as part of the promotion process. In the profile, it simply lists the level of the award and the date it was approved. In the case of a group award, the award is notated as "(group)". It does not reflect how large or small the group is. I suppose this means that if you simply develop a knack for showing up at the right place at the right time, you can really look like an all-star employee ... without expending any actual effort. The cost to the process, however, will extend long after the awards ceremony.

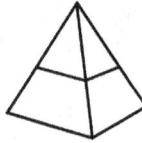

Here is the lesson:
Awards are incredibly useful tools to reward employees for their efforts and to show respect to the receiver. As a leader you need to take care to differentiate the assignments and then pay attention to the effort put in so you can nominate appropriate employees for appropriate awards. When nominating employees, it is okay to ask for input to ensure you get the story right from the employee's perspective, but make sure YOU as the leader take ownership of the nomination. Be careful with group awards: only give them to small groups (fewer than ten) who actually work as a team.

REFERENCES

O'Flaherty, S., Sanders, M. T., & Whillans, A. (2021, March 29). *Research: A little recognition can provide a big morale boost.* Harvard Business Review. https://hbr.org/2021/03/research-a-little-recognition-can-provide-a-big-morale-boost

Pink, D. H. (2009). *Drive: The surprising truth about what motivates us*. Riverhead Books.

Waxman, S. (1999, March 21). *The Oscar acceptance speech, by and large it's a lost art*. Washington Post. www.washingtonpost.com/wp-srv/style/movies/oscars/speeches.htm

Chapter 14

Collaboration

The spotlight is brighter when you share it

Take a minute and think of some of the most successful, longest-running television shows. Okay, there are soap operas, which have been around for decades, and then there are some of the longest running, most beloved comedies: *M*A*S*H*, *Friends*, *The Big Bang Theory*. What is one of the things these shows have in common with soap operas? They all had ensemble casts. They did not rely on a single "star" but rather focused on a group who shared the spotlight.

Soap operas take the idea of ensemble to a completely new level, since the character is sometimes more important than the actor playing the character. I remember once when I was at home with the flu in seventh or eighth grade. I was flipping through the television channels and came across an episode of *Days of Our Lives*. As I was watching, the following words appeared on the screen, "The part of [I cannot remember the character. Come on, it was a long time ago] is now being played by [whoever the new actor is]." I was stunned: they just replaced the actor and kept running with the story.

A good bureaucracy is very much like that. When an employee leaves or retires, a bureaucracy does not end that storyline, close that office, and open a new one on a different track; instead, it simply replaces the employee. Okay, in the case of senior-level management, replacing the employee, such as a cabinet secretary, agency administrator, or CEO, may not be simple, but for most of us, we leave, and we are replaced.

In fact, in my line of work, because we rotate every two to three years, we introduce ourselves for the first few weeks in a new assignment as, "Hi, I'm Chris, I'm the new Lisa" (or whomever you replaced). When I was replaced, my replacement spent a couple of weeks introducing himself as, "Hi, I'm Brian, I'm the new Chris." It's kind of like a running joke.

One of the reasons that a bureaucracy works is because it is an ensemble cast. By its very nature, it cannot fail just because of the departure of one person. As bureaucrats, we joke that we are replaceable and that the machine will keep running long after we leave. One of the duties of a mid-level, and even senior level, leader in a bureaucracy like this is to develop the talent at

DOI: 10.1201/9781003650454-17

the level below you (see Chapter 12) so that upper management can replace you as you move up (or out of) the pyramid. One of the most effective ways to show that you are ready for the next level is to make it apparent that you are capable of leading and developing other leaders.

Sometimes, though, individuals forget this. They may believe themselves highly important and believe that the most effective way to be promoted and make it to the next level is to show upper management that they are very important. This is a trap that many leaders fall into, including me from time to time.

This type of individual makes sure that if there is going to be a chance for recognition, they will be there in front to accept it. If there needs to be interaction with senior management, they will handle that interaction, even if a lower-level employee who is working on a given program might be fully capable and more knowledgeable about the topic in question. They are the supervisor, so they will be the "face and voice of the office: anything sent from this office to higher management will come from me, any questions from higher management will be directed to me."

If the upper management is happy, this individual is ready to take the credit for being such an outstanding leader. If upper management is unhappy, this individual is ready to place the blame on their subordinates, where they believe it rightly belongs because the subordinates have failed in the responsibility to make the supervisor look good to upper management. They seem to have confused the saying that a mark of a good leader is one who "shares the credit but takes the blame."

There was an episode in my mid-level 1 assignment where a more senior manager had questions, and I had the answers. As I knew this senior manager personally from another office where we had worked together, I gave him the answers. Boy, did I hear about that from my supervisor.

My supervisor pulled me into his office, closed the door, and told me that I was not to speak to higher management without going through him ever again, or he would write me up for insubordination and make sure to document my inability to follow the chain of command in my annual personnel review. Had I given the wrong answer? No, that was not the point. My job was to give my supervisor the answer so that HE could pass it up the chain. When it came time for award nominations, he made sure his name was on the list for a big one. Those of us who worked for him generally had to hope that someone else was going to nominate us because unless you were one of his "favored" employees, who had made him look particularly good in front of upper management, you might as well forget about it.

Contrast this to one of my managers in my assignment immediately after that one, mid-level 2. Let's call this supervisor Peter. Peter thought of himself as the star of the show. Though he was less radical about this than my mid-level 1 supervisor, it was still apparent. If you needed to brief upper management on an issue, Peter would usually "take care of it." Occasionally, he would let you come along, but he would still do most of the talking, even if you had more of the information. When a new operations chief for our worksite showed up and needed to get the new arrival briefing, Peter made sure that he was the one who gave it, without any assistance from anyone else, even though the rest of us gave this briefing on a weekly basis and he never gave it to anyone else. And then there was the time that the director (also known as the principal deputy assistant secretary) of our organization came for a site visit.

Peter was very excited by the opportunity to impress the big boss. He tried to take care of all the details himself, not even using the expertise and experience of our administrative assistant to help with the scheduling. He worked on the schedule for two weeks, but did not clue the rest of us into the plans until the day before the visit. About a week before the visit, one of my subordinates came to me in confidence and said, "Hey, Peter is having me arrange a cocktail reception for the director, but he is not planning on inviting anyone from the office, only outside contacts. I have told him he should invite the rest of the staff, but he does not want to. What should I do?" Because even though I, as the supervisor in line between Peter and the rest of the staff, had not heard about this yet, I told the employee to please go ahead and try to correct my supervisor's course and make sure the office personnel were added to the list and that I would speak to him as well.

Finally, on the day before the visit, Peter let us know what the schedule for the director's visit would be. Included in the schedule was the reception I had been warned about. The invitations had already been sent, and none of us were on the list. My staff was furious, and I had my opportunity to bring up the topic, so I asked him privately after the meeting, "Hey, why aren't any of us on the list for the reception?" Peter responded that it was just a small reception and that there was not a lot of money in the budget to host it, so he only was inviting outside contacts and a couple of other supervisors at the worksite who were at his level.

On the day of the visit, an employee from the protocol section who had helped arrange the reception told Peter that not enough people had RSVP'd, and the crowd was going to be thin. At four o'clock, three hours before the reception, Peter walked around to me and each of my subordinates and sheepishly said, "You don't have to come. I know it is late and you might have other plans, but if you want to come to the reception tonight, you can." As if any of us would have missed it. I mean, this reception was for one of the highest-level people in our organization! We all wanted a chance for him to notice us and our efforts on behalf of the organization!

I cannot think of a single legitimate reason why the staff would not have been invited to this reception. The only reason I can give is that Peter wanted to make sure the focus was on himself so that he could take the spotlight and make sure he was center stage, with the rest of us off in the wings. This is not leadership.

On the other hand, I can think of three very good reasons, from a leadership perspective, to invite the staff:

1) If indeed there is a budget shortfall, you go to the staff and say, "hey, the big boss is coming, and I want to have a reception for him. There is not a lot of money in the budget, but I want it to be a nice reception, so I am going to kick in "X" amount extra. I want you guys there too. Can you contribute something (bring something, contribute money, run the music, whatever) to make this something special?" This approach does a couple of things: you are up front about the circumstances of the event; you show you want to share the spotlight with them so that the big boss can recognize them too; and you get them to invest in the success of the event.

2) If you are having outside contacts, you want to make sure that your contacts are taken care of, and that they have someone to talk to and to host them at the event. If you are the only member of the office attending an event, you will not physically be able to entertain both the big boss and your other guests. By inviting the other members of your staff, you can solve this problem.

3) It is one thing to want to show the big boss how good you are at cultivating your local contacts. It is a whole other, much higher level, thing to show how good you are at cultivating your local contacts AND mentoring and developing your subordinate staff to be able to do the same.

Sharing the spotlight in leadership is not always just about making sure your staff gets the credit they deserve. Sometimes, it is also about giving them the chance to get in on rare, once-in-a-lifetime opportunities to show that you appreciate all their hard work.

During this same mid-level 2 assignment, President Barack Obama visited the city where I was working. When you work for the government, having a president visit, regardless of political party, is a BIG deal. The nature of my work meant that I, and my colleagues, had responsibilities that prevented us from gawking at the president as most of the other employees were able to do. In fact, even though the president held a meet and greet with personnel at the worksite, most of the people in my immediate team had responsibilities elsewhere at that time that prevented us from attending. I actually spent quite a bit of time during the visit within a few feet of the president, but the nature of my duties meant that I was typically facing the other direction: looking out, not in.

Getting a photo with a president, or any other world leader for that matter, is a coveted opportunity. Regardless of political affiliation, the simple fact that you are standing next to the president, getting your photo taken, is something special.

So, imagine this scenario for a minute: you are a supervisor in a small office of, say, half a dozen people. You and your four subordinates have been pulling 70- to 90-hour weeks for the last month, while Peter, who oversees this small office, has been putting in a little more than his regular hours. On the day of the visit, you get a call: "Hey, boss, I just saw the president's schedule. You won't believe this, but it has an item that has been added that says, 'Peter photo with POTUS.' It took place about a half hour ago."

It turned out that Peter spent days lobbying every White House staff he could corner into getting this onto the schedule. He knew everyone had been working their tails off, and he freely admitted this was the easiest presidential visit he had ever worked because he had such a good team taking care of the details for him. He also knew that two of the team members were at the venue where the photo-op would take place, and a third and fourth could break free to be there in time. No, not everyone would be available, but he could share this opportunity, right? He never even mentioned it to the rest of the staff. Instead, he brought along some of his outside contacts, so they could get their photo with the president too, thereby increasing his prestige in their eyes.

It did NOT go over well with the rest of the team.

Knowing that this had taken place and knowing that he had talked in general terms of wanting a photo, I casually asked Peter, "so did you get your photo with the president?"

"Yup, sure did," he replied. "It was great. I brought along a contact, who brought some of his staff and we all got photos with the president. Then, after us, he took some photos with the hotel staff. It was really nice." Then he asked, "Did you end up getting a photo with him?"

"No," I replied, "I was too busy working." Based on the tone of the conversation, it was clear that it never even crossed Peter's mind to invite his deputy or any of his other staff, even though his contact brought staff along himself.

Don't be that guy.

Instead, be the leader who shares the spotlight: the leader who develops your team members and offers chances for them to participate in unique opportunities. This will not always be possible. Sometimes there are restrictions put in place that invitations cannot be shared, but you can always ask the organizer to allow you to bring someone along.

My supervisor in my mid-level 2 assignment before Peter arrived was very good at this. When he had meetings with contacts or with the local business community, he always made sure to bring one of us along, rotating the opportunities so we all got a chance. My ambassador in my entry-level 1 position made it a point to rotate invitations to receptions through the entire staff so that each of us could participate and better understand the expectations of being a diplomat and host. My supervisor in my entry-level 1 position regularly sent me to brief the ambassador or their deputy on issues that I had knowledge of. The supervisor started the process by bringing me along to the briefings she was giving, then had me deliver the briefing while she was present, and finally allowed me to go on my own. The supervisor did this with all the members of our team.

Be that leader.

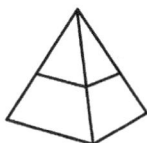

Here is the lesson:
As a leader, if you share the spotlight with your team, they will appreciate you and will work harder for you. If you hog the spotlight, block them out, and leave them in the dark, they will disparage your name. Remember, you are part of an ensemble cast, and in this bureaucratic ensemble, you need to develop the level below you so that they can take over for you as you move up. If you come across a once-in-a-lifetime opportunity, sharing it will strengthen your leadership, while keeping it to yourself will weaken you.

Part III

Leading organizations from wherever you stand

As President Dwight D. Eisenhower once said, leadership is

> the art of getting someone else to do something that you want done because he wants to do it, not because your position of power can compel him to do it, or your position of authority. A commander of a regiment is not necessarily a leader. He has all of the appurtenances of power given by a set of Army regulations by which he can compel unified action. He can say to a body such as this, "Rise," and "Sit down." You do it exactly. But that is not leadership.
>
> Eisenhower, 1954

Leadership is influence. Without being able to influence others, you will never be able to lead them. Sometimes this is positional—as you move up the pyramid, you will supervise and manage others—but as the words above demonstrate, this does not necessarily mean you lead them. Accordingly, the organizations you head up may vary in terms of size and scope. Keep in mind that a bureaucracy is made up of pyramids within pyramids. The organization you lead may simply be the sub-pyramid you are now supervising, or it could itself contain several sub-pyramids through which you are leading other supervisors.

It is true that at each level, there will be supervisory responsibilities: even the CEO of a company has supervisory duties over the vice presidents, and the board of directors has supervisory responsibilities over the CEO. Everybody reports to somebody.

As you move up the pyramid, the focus is less on supervising individuals and more on managing projects or programs: bringing together disparate parts to form a cohesive group for the accomplishment of a goal, smoothing out points of friction between various work styles, and shepherding the work unit to keep them on target. But you don't just want to "manage" supervisors in the levels of the pyramids below you. You want to "lead" them.

To be a leader of an organization, either a small organization within your agency, or the whole departmental pyramid, you need to influence them.

DOI: 10.1201/9781003650454-18

You need to have a vision that you can get others to buy into and want to achieve. You need to be able to work smoothly across jurisdictional boundaries and find ways to work around obstacles in your path. You need to be able to pull together different sections and suborganizations in appropriate combinations so that you can help them leverage each other's talents and efforts to achieve your (and your organization's) goals. You need to be in tune with your organization and deal with not just problem employees, but also problem supervisors and managers. You need to influence all levels of the organization: the ones in your direct reporting chain, and all the chains that feed into yours.

This is not always easy, and there will be defeats and setbacks. However, if you keep working at it and manage to accomplish the transition into being an organizational leader, the rewards can be amazing.

The following chapters contain some examples of what you need to do to become an organizational leader. This is not an exhaustive list, nor will the examples contained here be applicable to all organizations. As you read the chapters, reflect on the lessons and how they apply to your present organization or agency and how they would apply to an ideal organization or agency if YOU were the leader. Then, where possible, take steps to lead the changes necessary in your current agency to reflect the ideal you envision.

And here is a secret: even entry- and mid-level employees can lead entire departmental pyramids. I know, I have done it. Several times. To be successful, you need to be able to navigate and influence the pyramid.

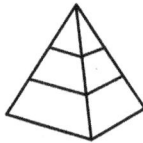

REFERENCE

Eisenhower, D. D. (1954). *Remarks at the Annual Conference of the Society for Personnel Administration.* National Archives www.eisenhowerlibrary.gov/eisenhowers/quotes

Chapter 15

Communicating up the pyramid

We need to feed the beast, but we try to give it bites it can chew

As a mid-level bureaucrat, one of the things I was expected to do was write reports and review reports of my subordinates as they moved up the chain. There are several schools of thought on report writing, but I boil them down into the following categories, based on lessons from "Goldilocks and the Three Bears": overly thorough, overly concise, and just right.

There is a move afoot to focus on "executive" writing, trying to get a point across in as few words as possible while leaving the details aside. In my agency, decision papers for senior leaders were supposed to be no longer than two pages, in 14-point font, double-spaced.

Read that sentence again, please. That's right, it does not give you much room to develop your argument, list the pros and cons, or explore alternatives. What it gives you is the opportunity to present a "fait accompli," and hope that it gets approved. That is not to say appendices and attachments cannot back up the decision papers, but these are attachments to the decision paper itself and typically go unread.

The military has a concept that has been adopted by many corporations called BLUF: Bottom Line Up Front. It takes an introductory summary to the extreme. You get one sentence to capture the essence of the issue. The BLUF is supposed to be an attention grabber. Once you have the readers' attention, then you can explain a bit. Make sure to keep the explanation tight and on point as well. Because the BLUF concept has worked its way throughout the government and corporations, it is a good idea to practice it. In Table 15.1, I have provided some examples of how you may see this and ways to use it yourself.

DOI: 10.1201/9781003650454-19

Table 15.1

Examples of simple topics boiled down to a BLUF

Project Status Briefing	The project is 80% complete and is scheduled to finish on time.
Meeting Request	I am requesting to meet for 30 minutes on Tuesday to discuss the new client proposal for ABC company.
Incident Resolution	The fire alarm was triggered by popcorn left in a microwave. The building evacuation lasted 30 minutes. The all-clear has been given; normal work is resuming. No injuries reported.

Even complex topics can be boiled down to a BLUF

Seeking board approval for an acquisition	XYZ is a successful family company with a strong brand and a business model similar to our own. The owners are seeking to sell the company and retire. The successful acquisition of XYZ company will expand our presence in the mid-west market with rapid results and position us for significant long-term growth.
Seeking Resources for an IT Project	Investing $20,000.00 in the requested software will speed processing times by 40%, eliminate three redundant processes, and allow retirement of two legacy systems. Savings are projected to exceed the investment within two years.

This brings me to the crux of the issue: attention spans, which brings me back to the lessons of "Goldilocks." Often, because there is so much information that higher-level leaders must consider and be aware of, their assistants and gatekeepers impose the "executive" writing concept that forces authors to present their points concisely, sometimes too concisely. If you restrict the flow of information too much, you can miss critical points, counterarguments, and alternative solutions.

At the same time, without imposing restrictions on the length of memos, decision papers, and briefings, you will end up drowning in information, potentially delaying critical decisions. The key is to strike a balance. As Albert Einstein reportedly said, "Make things as simple as possible, but not simpler." I alluded to this in Chapter 12, in which I described my experience when I proposed a major change that would affect my entire agency and had a good supervisor who mentored me through refining my pitch for senior leadership, helping me shrink my presentation from 30 minutes to seven.

As a leader, you need to understand what that balance is. The organization (the beast) needs sustenance (information) to survive, but it needs to be fed in bites that it can chew: if the individual papers are too large or the overall volume is too great, the beast will choke and stop in its tracks. If the papers are too concise and there is not enough "meat" to them, then the beast will start to drift off course as it starts to suffer from a lack of protein.

While the balance must be tailored to the individual organization and even to the individual executive, I did have one leader who I think struck an excellent balance. His theory was that most issues could be easily addressed in five paragraphs: a summary, three body paragraphs, and a comment paragraph. If the issue was complex, he was willing to accept nine paragraphs. If there were multiple alternatives, he would accept 12 paragraphs. Unless the circumstances were highly unusual, he would not send a report forward that was longer than 12 paragraphs. He also wanted us to stick to five sentences per paragraph. Finally, he pointed out that the summary is the most important paragraph because most readers only look at the first paragraph—the summary paragraph (kind of like the BLUF concept).

What this leader understood, and what he was trying to impart to us, was that headquarters is drowning in information, and the longer a paper, the less likely it is to be read. His theory was that if headquarters wanted more information on any given topic, they would ask for it (is the appetite of the beast sated with what we gave it, or is it still hungry?).

There are lots of tools available to help you sharpen your writing. Many of them are artificial intelligence (AI) driven. Some will simply help you with proofreading (spelling, grammar, etc.). Others will completely summarize your message for you, give you a BLUF, or even take some input and write the whole draft for you. See Box 15.1 for more thoughts on this.

Box 15.1

A note on AI for drafters: Artificial intelligence, such as large language models (think ChatGPT, CoPilot, Gemini, etc.), can certainly help streamline and tighten your message. Be careful, though. Always proofread. Make sure your point has not been changed or lost in the revision process. Ensure necessary facts are still present and have not been replaced with AI "hallucinations." If you are asking AI to provide you a list of references, make sure you look up those references to ensure they actually exist and contain the information referenced. AI is a fantastic tool and time-saver, but it still needs the human-in-the-loop to review, confirm, and discern that the information provided is accurate and on-target.

It is important to understand that it is not just headquarters drowning in information. With email, the Internet, blogs, wikis, official and personal social networking tools, and so on, people in the field are also drowning in information. As the leader of a team or organization, you need to strike that balance as well. An overly concise message may be subject to interpretation, uneven application, and may cause confusion. Overly long, detailed, bureaucratese-filled messages will often be ignored ("oh wow, I don't have time to read this whole thing now, I will save it for ... never").

This is why I was so disappointed in one aspect of the office review we had during my mid-level 2 assignment. As mentioned in Chapter 11, in designing Directives, my colleagues and I had recognized the problem of the length of messages, rules, directives, and such, and we had worked very hard to strike a balance. We tailored our messages to our local situation, including the required information but not overloading it with the bureaucratic legalese that causes people to roll their eyes and ignore it. We worked to make our messaging concise yet informative, with links to the authoritative references in the policy manuals.

Unfortunately, the inspectors sent to review our program had a very different standard. They required us to replace our carefully drafted, balanced, concise versions of the policy statements with overly long, tedious, bureaucratese-filled rehashes of the department policy manual. Literally, they wanted us to copy as many as 15 pages of the department policy manual and issue that out as local guidance, on an annual basis.

From the Washington perspective, this accomplished what one of my supervisors phrased as the "13th commandment of bureaucracies: 'thou shalt cover thine own ass.'" The inspectors did not care if anyone actually read the policy. All they cared about was that if something went wrong, they could point to this atrocious document and simply say, "we told you so." Leadership failure.

On a couple of their documents, I could see the point. We had gone overly concise and by expanding what we had somewhat, we had a greater influence. But on many of their requirements, I disagreed strongly. There is, in my mind, never a need to super-copy multiple pages of a department policy to reissue it as a local policy. It is always going to be much better to put in a summary statement of the purpose and key points of the policy, backed up by a hyperlink to the full text. By issuing the statement this way, you are making the policy more accessible (more concise, gets the point across, and more likely to be read) and providing easy access to the full text for those who need it or are interested. You still accomplish the "13th commandment" mentioned above. and you do it in such a way that you have a greater chance of influencing your audience.

Here is the lesson:
As the leader, you need to gauge the right balance for information flow, both up to you and down from you. Both too little and too much detail can cause paralysis and hinder the decision cycle and information absorption rate. This impedes your ability to influence your audience. Strike the right balance and your audience will eat it up. We need to feed the beast, but we need to give it bites it can chew.

Chapter 16

Communicating vision

The problem with having a vision is getting others to see

Throughout my career I have experienced several times when I have made suggestions or recommendations yet have been unable to successfully sell my idea, only to see that idea come full circle and get implemented three to five years after I suggested it, except that someone else gets the credit for it. I am not saying that people are stealing my ideas and taking credit for them. I am just saying that I tend to see one or more steps ahead in a lot of areas. Sometimes I had the influence to lead the idea to fruition; other times I lacked that influence.

A lot of this comes back to my personality profile, INTJ, which I discussed in Chapter 3. I tend to make leaps of logic that may seem confusing or unconnected to other people, even when I am able to explain the connections. One reason is that I intentionally work to learn constantly from a wide variety of sources and genres. This sentiment is reflected by Walter Isaacson in the introduction to his book *The Innovators*, in which he writes, "I was struck how the truest creativity of the digital age came from those able to connect arts and sciences. They believed that beauty mattered." A few paragraphs later he ties this not just to the digital age, but also to other historical figures like Leonardo da Vinci and Albert Einstein, saying of the latter, "When Einstein was stymied while working out General Relativity, he would pull out his violin and play Mozart until he could reconnect to what he called the harmony of the spheres" (Isaacson, 2014, p. 4).

I do not claim the genius of Leonardo, Einstein, Steve Jobs, or others of that caliber, but I have found later in my adulthood that three of my core values are "explore, collaborate, teach." I like learning new things, and each thing I learn is a connection with other information I already have. I like to find communities of purpose to work with others to learn more. I like to teach what I have learned so that others may benefit from it (like writing this book). Interestingly, Isaacson comments on the idea of collaboration as well, explaining, "The main lesson to draw from the birth of computers is that innovation is usually a group effort involving collaboration between visionaries and engineers and that creativity comes from many sources" (Isaacson, 2014, p. 84).

DOI: 10.1201/9781003650454-20

I am perfectly willing to admit that there are few, if any, truly unique ideas in the world that only one person creates. This is especially true for problem-solving: given a puzzle with a set of facts, chances are that multiple people, if given the opportunity, will come up with similar or identical solutions. It is even plausible that multiple solutions may solve the puzzle, or at least parts of it.

Here is an example of what I mean. First, a little background. In my particular sub-pyramid of my department, we are required to test our skills in several areas three times a year. Testing is only offered at certain times throughout each month, so synchronizing when you are due for a test and when the testing is available is sometimes problematic. In an effort to solve this problem, on June 16, 2011, my organization issued a notice that said in sum that the database that keeps track of the scores and test dates has now been synchronized with the email system to send reminders for when you are next due to take your test and a link to the web page that gives the available testing dates.

Great. Perfect. But wait a minute, this idea sounds familiar ... didn't I suggest something along these lines several years ago?

As it turns out, I still have a copy of the email I sent with my suggestion; I also have a pretty clear recollection of how the email came about. I was having lunch with a couple of colleagues, and we were discussing the mandatory training and the hassle caused by having to remember when our certifications would expire and trying to balance scheduling the new testing with all our other commitments. There had to be an easier way.

As a backdrop, in addition to the testing of one skill set every four months, we are also required to take refresher training on several topics annually and an even larger set of refresher trainings every five years.

As we turned this topic around over lunch, I suggested that what we really needed to do was to link the new training certification database with our email system so that the database could send us reminders of when we were due for what and then allow us to schedule the training and have the database automatically add the appointment to our calendars. Everyone at lunch agreed this was a great idea, so I sent an email to a friend of mine who then happened to be the director of training. The email was dated June 14, 2007.

I never got a response to my idea, until almost exactly four years later when the broadcast notice went out announcing that a solution almost identical to the one I proposed was being implemented.

Am I saying that upper management has been considering and working on my solution for the last four years and that it was finally ready? No, I am betting that somewhere along the line, someone else, considering the puzzle and set of given facts, probably came up with a similar solution. The difference is that other person used their influence to sell it. Could I have done the same earlier? Probably, but I failed to follow up and did not adequately influence the process.

Selling an idea has five parts: the problem, the proposed solution, the timing of the proposal, the audience for the proposal, and your ability to influence that audience. All five of these things need to line up for your vision to become a reality. If you are missing any of these critical components, it is unlikely your idea will be implemented. Let's break it down:

The problem: First, is the problem you are trying to solve worth solving? Is it a minor inconvenience that is easy to work around, so it is not really worth tackling, or, at the other extreme, is the problem you are addressing so large that it is hard to truly define the scope and limits? If it is the former, regardless of how good your proposed solution is, most people will ignore it because the problem is not burdensome enough to correct. If it is the latter, then explaining the solution will likely lose and confuse your audience. In this case, a better strategy may be to break the larger problem into parts and address each separately. Some good examples of this are global warming, Social Security, and the economy; these are often referred to as "wicked problems." The best problems are the ones that cause enough inconvenience or pain that people want them solved, but no one has had the magic combination to do that yet. These problems and solutions may flow from simple, complicated, complex, or chaotic systems. These terms and examples of them are included in Table 16.1.

Table 16.1

Understanding simple, complicated, complex, and chaotic systems

System	Example(s)	Explanation
Simple	Light switch	Clear start and end point. Cause and effect relationship. Easily understood by looking at it.
Complicated	Internal combustion engine	Interconnected simple systems. Multiple variables. Can be traced and understood. While cause and effect is clear, not everyone can see it.
Complex	Weather, the stock market, AI	Systems with feedback loops and unpredictability. A cause can have multiple effects and minor adjustments can result in the emergence of unexpected consequences.
Chaotic	Double Pendulum, Global migration	The relationship between cause an effect is impossible to determine and rapidly shifting. No manageable patterns exist.

These examples are drawn from mechanics, systems engineering, nature, economics, and social sciences.

For more on these concepts in executive decision-making, see "A Leader's Framework for Decision Making" by David Snowden and Mary Boone, in Harvard Business Review. *https://hbr.org/2007/11/a-leaders-framework-for-decision-making*

The proposed solution: Does your solution have broad enough applicability to solve the problem for everyone or most everyone with the problem? Is the solution simple, elegant, and articulable, or is it a Rube Goldberg[1] contraption full of unnecessary moving parts? If your solution fixes the problem for a small subset of the population but not the majority or more, then you will have issues getting your audience to buy into it. Even worse, if your solution solves the problem for a small subset, but creates bigger problems for everyone else, you will face a lot of resistance. Finally, if you have trouble explaining the solution and influencing the decision-makers, it will never be implemented.

Timing: Is this a problem now, or in the future? Can your solution be implemented with available resources, or does some new process or technology need to be developed? Coming back to my proposal on the training reminders, when I made my suggestion, my sub-pyramid had about 1,100 people. It is now over 2,000. Additionally, when I made my suggestion, there were fewer training requirements, but these requirements grew over time, adding to the strain. When I sent my proposal, the problem had not grown complex enough to warrant much attention. My solution was spot on (as reflected in the broadcast announcement), but I was too far ahead of most people in realizing it would be a problem. My timing was off.

Audience and influence: Does the person you are proposing the solution to have the power to make the solution happen? You might recognize a key problem; you might have the perfect solution; or your timing may be perfect, but if you cannot find the right person or combination of people to sell your idea to, it will go nowhere. Sometimes, timing and audience combine; you have the right audience, but they are too preoccupied with other things to address the problem and solution you identified. On the other hand, perhaps you know the POSITION in the pyramid that you need to reach, but the PERSON in the position is not amenable to considering the issue, so you may need to wait until there is a new person in that same position.

So, what does all this have to do with leading organizations? If you identify the problem correctly and you come up with an appropriate solution, if the timing is right and you can sell your idea to the right audience, you can lead the entire pyramid through the necessary change, regardless of your actual level, rank, or grade. Leadership of this type is not dependent on the supervisory or managerial level; it is based on the ability to influence.

When I rotated from my Journeyman 1 assignment to Journeyman 2, I had not even reached mid-level yet, but I was put into a position to implement a vision that I had. I had recognized the problem and started to formulate the solution in my entry-level 2 job. In my first overseas assignment (entry-level 2), I was put in charge of updating the emergency plan for my worksite. I thought the methodology for accomplishing this task hindered crisis preparedness and emergency response rather than improving it, so I came up with new method of doing it to meet the objectives.

My supervisor supported my new method, but headquarters rejected it. Luckily, my supervisor told headquarters that this was our new plan, that we were sticking with it, and she encouraged me to keep refining my new methods. Other offices in our region heard about what I had done and asked if I could help them do the same, so I did. As this new process started to spread, headquarters slowly started to warm up to the idea.

When I rotated to my Journeyman 1 assignment, I continued this process, refining my concepts of how to create the emergency plans for the worksite and helping others do the same. In 2002, as I was lobbying for my next posting, I received a call from headquarters: senior management had realized the problem I was addressing in fact existed, and further, they had recognized the potential of my ideas and planned to create a position dedicated to fixing the problem. The caller asked me if I wanted the position. Hell yes! For three years, I had been advocating for my solution, word had been spreading, and I had earned a hallway reputation as someone with a good handle on both the problem and the direction we needed to go to solve it. It also helped that my supervisor from my entry-level 2 assignment used her influence to advocate for me and my solution.

The problem was, senior management did not want me to simply fix the part of the problem I was focused on; rather, they wanted me to fix the whole system, including how the worksites developed their plans and submitted them for approval.

My mandate was fourfold:

1) fix the backlog of plans waiting for review and publication,
2) streamline the process to eliminate future backlogs and get the plans published faster,
3) find a way to create better, more site-specific plans, and
4) create a process that made it easier to keep the plans up to date.

And, I had two years until I rotated again, so the project had to be substantially completed within 24 months. Plus, I had to coordinate and get approvals for everything I was going to do from all the other affected sections of the Department of Pyramids.

Suddenly, I needed a bigger vision! Luckily, I had parts of one and I found a couple of other people (collaborators!) with ideas that made my overall vision possible.

I finished mandate 1 (fix the backlog) within 90 days, which raised my credibility level with senior management. I accomplished mandate 2 (streamline the submission and publication process) within 180 days. By transforming some of our business processes, I managed to cut the processing time from submission to publication from an average of 140 days to an average of 15 days. Frankly, mandates 1 and 2 were the easy ones, I had the resources needed to accomplish the job, and I just needed to reprioritize the resources and change some business processes. In addition, these actions were internal to the team under my care. I therefore had positional influence, and as I described in Chapter 9, I was able to build the internal alliances I needed to bring them along.

Mandate 3 (create a framework and policy for better site-specific plans) required a radical leap: I proposed not just updating the current policy but completely replacing it with a new structure that was wholly different from anything the department had done before. Luckily, my success up to this point had given me access to senior management and the influence that I needed to sell my new concept. Just as luckily, senior management had come to recognize there was a problem, but had not been able to dedicate the resources themselves to riddle out a solution. Finally, though my solution was a radical departure from past practices, I was able to put together a simple, elegant, articulable explanation of it, with the help of my chain of supervisors that I described in Chapter 12. I was given the green light.

Mandate 4 (create a process for keeping these new plans up-to-date) was closely tied to Mandate 3 (create the framework and policy for better plans). I wanted both solutions to be implemented at the same time. I saw this as key to the overall success of the program. I wanted a web-based system that would generate a seamless emergency plan, by combining the boilerplate department-mandated guidance with the site-specific detail that was so critical to successful crisis preparedness and emergency response.

We had created a very basic version of the application on an internal basis to accomplish Mandate 2 (streamline the submission and publication process). I wanted to massively upgrade the software, take it to a whole new level, and make it the department-wide global standard. While the solution itself may have been complicated, I was able to explain it simply (as discussed in Chapter 15, feeding the beast in bites it could chew), which aided me in getting the ideas approved.

Just as the end of my two-year tenure approached, the final approvals for my new policy were given (I'll discuss how that worked in the next couple of chapters). Shortly thereafter, the software went live, and the policy was published. At age 32, with just eight years in my agency, from a journeyman-level position, I had led my department (not just my bureau, but the whole department) through a completely radical revision of how emergency plans would be created, updated, approved, and published for every worksite in the world.

As excerpted in Chapter 3, my performance review that year stated that my accomplishments were "perhaps the best example of transformational engineering the Department has enjoyed to date." I was also named the 2004 recipient of my department's Award for Innovation in the Use of Technology. Leadership is not tied to rank; it is a quality unique unto itself, grounded in vision and influence.

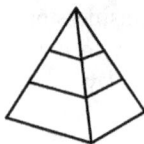

Here is the lesson:
You are not going to be able to sell every idea you have at the
time you have it. You must have all four factors to get your idea
implemented: a recognizable problem, a workable solution, the right
timing, an audience who can help you achieve your goals, and the
ability to influence them. If you are lacking any one of these factors,
you will not be successful. Persistence pays off. If you truly believe in
the problem and the solution you have identified, then you can keep
working on the timing and the audience until you find the right com-
bination to apply your influence. Regardless of your rank or position,
you can lead your organization through the necessary change.

Note

1   A Rube Goldberg contraption is a deliberately overengineered machine or process that performs a very simple task in a ridiculously complicated way. It's named after American cartoonist and inventor Rube Goldberg, who drew humorous illustrations of these types of absurdly complex devices in the early twentieth century. Fun fact: my son and I created one to open a door. The contraption involved a ladder, several ramps, a bucket on a rope and pulley, three balls, and a book. If I recall, it took more than a dozen steps to push open a door that was already ajar. Other examples can be found through online search engines and through the Rube Goldberg Institute at www.RubeGoldberg.org.

REFERENCE

Isaacson, W. (2014). *The innovators: How a group of hackers geniuses and geeks created the digital revolution.* Simon and Shuster.

Chapter 17

Navigating the pyramid

Leading up can be tough, try leading sideways first, then up

Remember, coalition building is not just for wars in the in the Middle East![1] You can accomplish a lot of business over a cup of coffee, if you know who to do business with.

There will be occasions when you need to accomplish a task, and you need upper management to support it, but you are not able to gain traction with them to get that support. Maybe they are too busy to listen to you. Maybe your presentation of the problem and the solution is just not quite sinking in. Maybe upper management would be receptive, but you need first to get through the levels of management between them and you. So what do you do?

There are a couple of ways in which you can attempt to influence the issue laterally, or horizontally, to build needed support to move the issue up to the decision-makers. Two of the most effective ways of finding this support are creating a grassroots campaign and utilizing the concept of six degrees of separation. I used both techniques to lead my agency through several changes, even though I was at a mid-, or lower, level.

The two major differences between the two methods are time and access. A grassroots campaign may take a while to develop but does not require access to key decision-makers. A six-degrees strategy may result in a faster idea-to-implementation cycle, but it requires you to be able to understand and navigate the necessary relationships to advance the issue.

There is a reason that grassroots campaigns are so effective. Whether they are for a politician or a cause, grassroots campaigns are very useful. They create buzz and interest: many people start talking about the issue. Suddenly, instead of just hearing a single voice, upper management is hearing about the issue from multiple sources, making them more likely to take an interest themselves.

One example of a grassroots campaign are the mechanisms I mentioned in the introduction through which employees could post ideas or solutions to perceived problems directly to upper management. These suggestions go

DOI: 10.1201/9781003650454-21

straight to the top of my agency. Management even added two features to this suggestion site: like/dislike buttons, and a polling feature.

You get one vote with the like/dislike feature, so you cannot pad the count. You can also change your vote if you reconsider the issue or are swayed by the thread of comments posted beneath the original submission. When I reviewed a sampling of the ideas offered, some had failed to gain much attention, only resulting in a few likes or dislikes, but some of the ideas were liked, or in some cases disliked, by hundreds or even thousands of employees. Now, in this system, the likes and dislikes cancel each other out, so if you have five likes and four dislikes, the score is +1. Imagine what this means when you see a score of +223 or –178: this means that the overwhelming majority of people who reviewed this submission feel strongly about it. It gives you a good sense of where the overall community stands.

Polling works much the same way, except you get more options. For instance, there may be a suggestion that a new service needs to be added to improve efficiency. Instead of just indicating that you like or dislike the idea, you can actually express how often you think you would use the service: always, frequently, sometimes, rarely, or never. This information gives upper management a better sense of the playing field before they commit funding to an idea that may have seemed popular but ends up being a dud.

Sadly, in the shift in leadership over the years, this system went into disuse, and then disappeared completely. You don't need software to create a grassroots campaign; however, you can always do it the old-fashioned way: talk to people. Try to build a coalition and buzz around an idea.

The other method I recommend is similar to the party game called "Six Degrees of Kevin Bacon," which is based on the theory of "six degrees of separation." The theory is that you can connect with anyone in the world through six other people or fewer. The goal is to find the right combination of connections. In the Kevin Bacon game, someone names a movie that Kevin Bacon is not in. You then think through the list of actors in the movie and the other movies they have filmed, then the other actors in those movies and so on until you arrive at the combination that gets you to a movie in which Kevin Bacon appeared.

The overall six degrees of separation theory works the same way. Imagine you want to get information to a senior-level leader or decision-maker. You may not know that person, but according to the theory, each person is only six or fewer social connections away from ANYONE else on the planet. The key is to find the right combinations of connections. In fact, researchers proved this theory all the way back in 2008 (Smith, 2008).

This concept is important because if you have an idea you are trying to move to upper management and you cannot gain their attention, you must find the right combination of people to connect with, to get the idea to the level of management that you want.

So instead of trying to go straight up the pyramid, first go sideways to someone else at your level who has a contact, to move the idea forward to a contact they have. The goal is to then stairstep sideways, then up, until you reach the level you need to truly influence. Sometimes, you may only need to go up a couple of levels in the pyramid, while other times, you may need to go way up.

One problem you have with either of these methods (grassroots and six degrees) is the loss of control. As you involve other people in selling your idea, these other people may put their own spin or emphasis on it. Like the game of telephone, each time the idea gets passed from one person to the next, it may be changed slightly (or significantly), so by the time the idea finally reaches the end, the concept is completely different from what you originally proposed, and it may no longer address the issue you were targeting. The other issue, of course, is unscrupulous people taking credit for the idea. There are really only two ways to deal with these issues: 1) find a way to define the problem and solution simply and concisely, and 2) try to ensure that the idea is strongly associated with you. The best way to guard against these problems is ensure your communications about the idea are in writing and not just passed along verbally.

I have tried to use both techniques for advancing ideas with a mix of success. When I was working on redesigning the emergency planning policy for my department, there were several new concepts I wanted to introduce that ran into resistance simply because they were new. I hit a brick wall when I tried to move the idea up the chain.

In some of these cases, I simply moved sideways, spoke with my colleagues in another division who were also stakeholders in the project I was working on, and convinced them of the merits of the idea. My colleagues were then able to advance the idea up a level in their chain, who laterally pushed the idea back to my chain of command. Since the idea was now coming from an equal level of management (albeit in a different division), my management looked at the suggestion more seriously and usually accepted it.

Sometimes, I needed a broader consensus, so instead of working with just one other division, I worked with three, four, or more, creating a mini grassroots campaign for the idea. The personal relationships I built through this process shortened the idea-to-implementation cycle each time we went through the exercise because I learned which issues were near and dear to the hearts of my colleagues, and because I respected their points of view. I also learned the degrees of separation and which chains were either the shortest or were longer but more useful for the issue at hand.

There are two major pitfalls to either one of these methods for advancing ideas: getting the reputation of being an instigator and falling on your sword for an unimportant issue. You want the reputation of an innovator, someone who sees issues both strategically and tactically, coming up with solutions to problems on the horizon that others may not have even recognized yet.

Being seen as an innovator is great and as your reputation grows, you will be called on more and more by senior management and increase your chances for promotion and/or to work on more complex problems.

If you are not careful with how you advance your ideas, though, you will be seen as an instigator, someone who stirs up trouble over minor issues and becomes a thorn in management's side. In this case, you may be shunted aside and ignored, even when your advice is exactly right. Your chances to work on major issues will be slim, just like your chances for promotion.

Falling on your sword over a minor issue is the other pitfall. Remember, you want credit for your ideas and you want to maintain some semblance of control over the idea-to-implementation cycle. As such, you want to make sure the idea is strongly associated with you. This may lead you to overinvest your credibility in a particular issue or cause, and when the idea flops, you go down with it. It can take a long time to recover from this, both psychologically and for your reputation. Be careful about the ideas that you advance, both for yourself and for others. If you are getting a lot of resistance as you work the six degrees theory or as you try to start a grassroots campaign, it may be simply that your timing is off, or the idea is unworkable. Stop before you impale yourself.

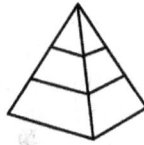

Here is the lesson:
Sometimes you may have an idea that you believe has merit, but your chain of command is resistant to the idea. Two ways to advance the idea in the face of resistance are to create a grassroots campaign or to find the right combination of people to help sell the idea. Be careful in using these methods and reserve them only for ideas that you strongly believe in. If you encounter resistance in implementing these methods, reassess the timing and the idea to avoid damaging your reputation.

Note

1   In the buildup to the first Gulf War, after Iraq had invaded Kuwait in 1990, President George H. W. Bush focused intently on building a coalition of allies who would participate in various ways to force Iraq back out of Kuwait. Operation Desert Shield was designed to prevent further incursions into other countries, such as Saudi Arabia. The coalition building was seen as a diplomatic and military triumph. Later in 2003, when President George W. Bush (son of George H. W.

Bush) was concerned about a weapons of mass destruction program that many in the intelligence community believed was a serious ongoing threat to global stability, he followed his father's model and created what he called the "coalition of the willing" of approximately four dozen countries who participated in some way (most not providing military forces). This "coalition of the willing" term has since been used for other military conflicts such as countries supporting Ukrainian resistance to Russia's invasion. These are not a formal alliance, such as NATO, nor a formal international organization such as the United Nations.

REFERENCE

Smith, D. (2008, August 2). *Proof! Just six degrees of separation between us*. The Guardian. www.theguardian.com/technology/2008/aug/03/internet.email

Chapter 18

Leveraging project teams

"I am not a committee"

There is a great exchange in the classic Star Wars movie *The Empire Strikes Back* in which Han Solo is rushing to fix the Millennium Falcon so he and his companions can escape from the imperial forces. Princess Leia offers a suggestion that she believes may be helpful, to which Han responds, "I don't have time to discuss this in committee," prompting a retort from Leia, "I am not a committee!" (Kershner, 1980).

Committees have gotten a bad rap in recent years, accused of creating groupthink, slowing down processes, and generally creating inefficiencies. To that I say, it is not the committee's fault; rather, it is the committee chair's fault for showing a lack of leadership. These days, committees are known by lots of different names: project teams, working groups, panels, task forces, councils, and so on. Ultimately, it is a group of people brought together, typically from different disciplines to assess and find solutions to one or more issues.

A committee is a mini bureaucracy within itself, but one in which the reporting chains are flattened, which makes strong leadership even more important. Throughout my career, I have had the pleasure (or misfortune; you choose) of both serving on and chairing several committees for different projects. Throughout this experience, I learned quite a bit about running committees.

There are a couple of things to keep in mind when you are starting up or taking over responsibility for running a committee. First, what is the purpose of the committee or working group? I am not talking about the vision statement or the motto or slogan of the group, I am asking what is the true, actual purpose that you are trying to accomplish? Second, and this follows closely from the first, what is the composition of the committee and does the composition contribute to the purpose?

One of the reasons that committees get a bad reputation is because they experience drift: they start with a particular purpose, but over time, they shift their focus, sometimes subtly, sometimes abruptly. This can happen because the original purpose was achieved, yet the group continues to meet

DOI: 10.1201/9781003650454-22

out of inertia, or because the group lacks the leadership necessary to keep the participants focused. It is critical to define the goal of the committee, to stay focused on that goal, and once the goal is achieved, to dissolve the committee. There is some room for standing committees, although the goal of these needs to be particularly well defined and they should only be convened when an issue arises that reaches the threshold of the defined purpose.

Another reason committees gain a bad reputation is because too many members walk out of the meetings publicly asking why they were there in the first place, or why someone else was present. The composition of a committee needs to be examined on two levels: what organizations should be present, and which individuals from those organizations best represent the purpose of the committee. Sometimes, a higher-level decision-maker is needed. More often you simply need knowledgeable mid-level or even journeyman-level personnel who can provide input, absorb discussion, and take key points back to decision-makers.

When examining which organizations need to be present, I again recommend the lessons of Goldilocks and the three bears: if the committee is too small, you will miss valuable input; if it is too large, you will get bogged down in trying to accommodate everyone; therefore, you need to strike the right balance. Do not be afraid to let people know that you have a committee and that they are not invited. One of two things will happen in this case: either they will thank you for not continuing to burden them with additional tasks, or they will make a case for why they should be included and then you can invite them to sit in on a particular session or join the committee.

Interestingly, one of the best committees I was involved in was started specifically because someone was trying to derail a project I was working on. In my Journeyman 2 position, in addition to updating the emergency planning policy, I was responsible for putting together requirements for a new software application we designed to process these emergency plans, including drafting the new plans, putting them through a review and approval process, publishing the approved versions, and then keeping them updated.

One of the senior managers in the IT department felt it would be far simpler to rely on templates developed in a word-processing program, much as had been done up to that point. I disagreed. I had a couple of specific goals, and I had worked closely with the IT team to develop those goals into the requirements document that would be used to help the software engineers write the code for the program.

Even though I had support from my agency's senior management, this IT manager did not believe in my vision, so he tried to slow me down in the bureaucratic structure of a committee. He told me, "Well, we are starting a new concept in the IT section: starting with your program, all future application developments need to have a formal 'stakeholders focus group' convened to review the development and approve it. Let me know when that is done and then we will see about you moving forward."

The manager's goal was to get this thing so bogged down in a committee that it would be months or years before I could move it forward, by which time I would rotate out of my job and the project could die. I took this situation as an opportunity for bureaucratic efficiency: to create greater buy-in for my concept across a larger swath of the agency, which could then smooth the roll-out process when it was done. Instead of fighting this "stakeholder's focus group" initiative, I embraced it.

Luckily, I had been working with the key stakeholders for months as we hashed out the new policies that this software was designed to support. Let me provide a little more context.

When you work for a large bureaucracy, no one single entity will have complete control over major processes. There are going to be a lot of offices and subunits from disparate parts of the agency that are going to be responsible for different pieces. For instance, while I was responsible for the overarching Emergency Planning Policy, there was another office responsible for training, one responsible specifically for fire prevention and response, another responsible for monitoring developments that might cause the implementation of the plans, and so forth.

To get my new policy approved and published, I had to get all these entities, plus all the offices responsible for the various geographic regions to sign off. As it happened, there was a committee, which met on an as-needed basis, to coordinate these various offices and review what everyone was doing on a strategic basis. The Crisis Management and Training Oversight Committee was cochaired by the Office of Crisis Management Support and the Crisis Management Training Office, which were in separate divisions of my agency.[1]

Prior to one of the meetings, I met ahead of time with the key players on the committee, explained my project to them, and got them to support my initiatives. One of the *key* steps I took was to ensure that I had, from each office, a dedicated point of contact who had the authority to make minor decisions and the ability to get their senior managers to review and make major decisions. This way, when I needed input or approval on policy language, I could just send it to the right combination of people from my address book.

With this commitment in hand, I asked the cochairs of the committee to call a meeting so we could detail the project to the rest of the group. After explaining my project, I then hit the members with what I needed from them: a designated point of contact from each office. As we went around the table, the cochairs and other key members of the committee that I had worked with ahead of time each voiced their support and named who would be the point of contact, and with this momentum, every office represented on the committee fell into line.

So, catching back up to the Stakeholders Focus Group, I already knew and had developed relationships with the exact combination of people I would need for this group. Within a couple of days, I had contacted each of them and explained that we were moving into the software development phase of the project and that I needed their support as a Stakeholders' Focus Group. We had our first meeting the next week.

Prior to the first meeting, I sent all the invitees a copy of the agenda of the group and a copy of the *charter*. Yes, I drafted a formal charter that outlined the goals and parameters of the group, so everyone understood why they were there, the expectations, and the end goal. Each committee member was required to sign the charter and abide by it. One of the articles of the charter was the structure, listing me as committee chair. Keep in mind that I was in my Journeyman 2 assignment. Most of the members of the committee significantly outranked me, but they all agreed in writing that I was in charge of this project and group. As I said before, you can take a leadership role in your organization, even if you are not yet in a senior position.

Whenever the focus group met, I sent an agenda a couple of days ahead of time. I also worked hard to keep the meetings to under an hour, and to schedule them around the times of the shuttle bus that ran between the various buildings my agency works from in the Washington, DC, metro area. These were the days before the convenience of MS-Teams, Zoom, Slack, and other web messaging and meeting platforms.

These steps all showed that I valued the time of my committee members, which they appreciated and better ensured their participation. At the first meeting, as we reviewed the purpose of the committee and the charter, I had each participant introduce themselves to the group and briefly explain which "stake" they held, so everyone understood why they themselves were there and why everyone else was there. When there were major decisions, such as acceptance of the requirements for the software, the focus group members signed a written copy, so there would be no question as to what had been agreed to.

Instead of being bogged down in committee for months or years as the IT supervisor had hoped, I had the initial concept agreed to at the second meeting and the requirements signed off in under a month, allowing the project to move forward. Also, as suggested changes were offered and incorporated, we made the final product better and guaranteed the buy-in necessary to make the project successful.

Rather than becoming a major stumbling block and derailing my project as the IT manager hoped, my implementation of the Stakeholders Focus Group became the model that my bureau used. Moreover, the senior IT managers worked with me to assist several other groups in completing their own processes (growing my influence outside my original sphere, which came in handy later in my career).

I learned a lot from this process, and I was able to implement those lessons into other committees I oversaw.

I have also been part of a couple of committees that were not as successful. At the same time as I was running my own Stakeholders Focus Group, another committee was formed to review an existing piece of software that was not achieving the goals that the agency wanted.

The person selected to chair this committee was the head of my division, so he asked me to sit in for a couple of meetings to see if I could get the group to move forward. Unfortunately, the committee was not well structured. There was no agenda for the meetings, the attendees were not at a level that could commit to the decisions of the group, and the group never got to the core issues they were supposed to resolve, instead focusing on protecting the turf of each individual office.

In the end, the group agreed that the software was not ideal, but after months of meetings they had been unable to figure out a way to address the problems, so they simply left it in place. I had suggested to the committee chair that he might try implementing some of the lessons I had learned from my own process, but he was not a strong enough leader to follow through and do it, even though he was a senior manager. As I pointed out in the opening of Part III of this book, rank and seniority do not bestow leadership ability; leadership is a separate quality itself.

In my mid-level 2 assignment, I had the opportunity to lead a different kind of committee. I was asked to run for the board of directors for our local Employees Recreation Association. When I was elected to the board, I was then asked to be the president of the Association and chairman of the board. I reluctantly accepted both. I say reluctantly because I was concerned about how much of my own time this responsibility would consume and because of the scope of the Association. At the time, the Employee Association ran a cafeteria, a small store, two snack bars, a swimming pool, a gas station, and offered numerous services to our members. We had revenues just short of one million dollars a year and employed about 20 people. This was not just a little employee association; it was a small business, albeit not for profit.

One of the things that often happens when you run a successful nonprofit, is people have all kinds of ideas on how to spend the profits. Also, since the board was elected by the membership and not handpicked by me, I had no control over the composition of the group.

It turned out that the leadership lessons I had learned in running other committees applied directly to this one. We already had a charter, the bylaws that governed the association. Due to the amount of business and the number of issues that we dealt with, I determined that the board should meet monthly, with virtual meetings via email if there was a time-sensitive issue that could not wait for a regular meeting. The week before the meeting, I emailed the board members with a date, time, and location of the proposed upcoming meeting, a draft agenda, a request for additional agenda items, and the minutes from the previous meeting. The email included a request for confirmation of attendance so I could ensure we would have a quorum. At the meetings, I always brought printed copies of the agenda listing who would be leading the various discussions. While we did not always start exactly on time, we were generally pretty close because I had made a point to mention promptness at the first meeting we had. Also, we had to finish in our allotted time because of commitments the other board members had.

As the chair, I had to shape the flow of the meeting. Just because you have an agenda does not mean the meeting will stay on track. Sometimes, discussions will start down tangents and eat up valuable time that could be used more productively. Some tangents are useful, and others are red herrings[2] you chase and chase, but they never amount to anything useful. The key, as the leader, is to be able to determine which tangents are necessary and productive (even if it means tabling another part of the agenda for a later meeting), and which are the red herrings that will simply eat up time. Also, on this board, as with any committee, I had some members who were more vocal and vociferous, ensuring their opinions were heard. Others had very valuable views but were unable to break through the diatribe. As the leader, I had to control the exorbitant members and give the quiet ones a chance to speak.

I cannot take credit for the success of the Association. We had an excellent general manager, wonderful staff, and an outside financial consultant to keep our books straight and offer us advice on how best to spend our profits for the good of the community. My role was to ensure that we operated within the guidelines of the bylaws and lead the board in making decisions that were most beneficial to the membership. There were several proposals that we, as the board, had to decline for one or both reasons. Some of the ideas sounded great: but as the leader, I had to ensure that these excellent proposals were framed in the context of our boundaries, to ensure the proper stewardship of our organization.

Committees are organizations. You can use your membership on a committee to hone your own leadership skills and to learn lessons that will help you in a broader leadership context. If you are lucky, you will get a chance to chair a committee, and if you perform well, you can continue to improve your "hallway reputation," leading to bigger opportunities. The size of the organization you lead is not important; it may be a small committee, a mid-sized company, or a large government agency. The important point is to ensure you are ready to lead when given the chance.

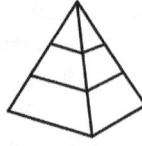

Here is the lesson:
Committees can be a useful tool, if you use them prop-
erly. Committees need a strong chair and the right balance of
representatives. Having a charter that outlines the purpose, goals,
and structure of the committee can help streamline the process,
create buy-in, and limit mission creep or drift. It is also important to
call meetings only when they are needed, keep them as short as prac-
ticable, and have an agenda to keep everyone on track.

Notes

1 Diplomatic Security (which housed the emergency planning program) and the Foreign Service Institute (which housed the Office of Crisis Management Training) were separate Bureaus, each headed by an assistant secretary, that fell under the undersecretary for management. Crisis Management Support (later renamed Crisis Management and Strategy) fell under the executive secretary, which is an assistant secretary equivalent, but reports directly to the deputy secretary and the secretary. Refer to Figure 0.1 to better understand the levels of management here. For reference, in that graphic, my position fell in the lower mid-level branch chief band. Yes, I was driving this process from that far down the pyramid. This is not to brag, but merely to illustrate what is possible.
2 Red herrings are a classic logical fallacy in which someone brings up a topic intended to mislead or distract from the original topic of conversation or purpose.

REFERENCE

Kershner, I. (Director). (1980). The Empire strikes back [Film]. Lucasfilm; 20th Century Fox.

Chapter 19

#RONI

Return on Network Investment

It is said that half of success is just showing up. In many ways that is true. If you don't show up, you have no chance of succeeding. The question then becomes, as a leader and manager, what should I show up for? The answer is, as much as you can: birthdays, funerals, weddings (if you are invited), appreciation parties, award ceremonies, and so forth. You have no idea how well it will be reflected on you and how much your influence can grow just because you show up.

As I said in Part 1 of this book, I am an introvert. It takes serious effort and energy for me to motivate myself to go to large social gatherings. I do it because it is important. It is important not just to be seen, but also because people will remember you were there and that you made the effort to show up. They will appreciate that, and your credibility meter will rise a bit.

It may not always be easy, especially when the event is unscheduled and conflicts with other plans that you have. It is important to show up, though, for two reasons: the impact your presence may have, in both the short and the long term, and because you never know what you may learn.

Have you ever shown up for work on Monday morning to hear everyone chattering about an event they all attended over the weekend that you were invited to, but chose not to go to? Did you feel that pang of regret? I've been there. I can come up with all kinds of excuses not to go to things. I am tired. It is raining. I want to spend time with my family. There is a movie I want to stream. For me, it is harder to come up with a reason *to go*. After feeling like the odd man out on Monday morning, though, my excuse for going is now often, "because I don't want to miss something." Some may call this FOMO, or fear of missing out. Taken to an extreme, it is not good. But really, we all need a little FOMO in our lives because it leads us to opportunities to build relationships and influence.

Opportunities come from people; the more people you know, the more relationships you cultivate, and the more opportunities you will encounter. I refer to this as Return on Network Investment, or RONI. This is like the ROI, or return on investment, used in business or finance, but is not about money; it is about people. Since I left government service, I have had the opportunity to attend several industry conferences, growing my network substantially outside. This growing network has both allowed me to find opportunities for consulting work, speaking engagements, podcast appearances, for publishing articles, and even for writing this book. Just as important, building my network also allowed me to introduce people I know to each other and support them in their efforts. This again builds my credibility, strengthens my network connections, and provides further RONI. As I reflect on my time in my bureaucracy, I see the parallels there too.

Relationships are critically important. Maintaining relationships takes effort. People do notice when you put in the effort. Do you need to be at an event from beginning to end? Not really: you can balance your commitments, and your energy. Even showing up for a little while will help, and again, you never know what you might learn.

By attending social events with my colleagues, I have gained insight into their relationships. I am not talking about romantic relationships, but friendships and collaborative relationships that you may not be aware of in a work setting. This knowledge can be useful because it may allow you to put together committees or project groups in ways that you had not otherwise anticipated. It also helps you figure out the six degrees of separation mentioned in Chapter 17.

It is not only parties and receptions. A guy from another office asked me to go SCUBA diving with him. I enjoy SCUBA diving, but I was pretty tight for time. I set up the dive anyway. On the drive out to the dive site, we had about an hour to talk. I learned a lot about his impressions of his office and its leadership, and his office's views of my office. By the end of the day, I had made another ally and had insights into how some of the ways my office operated were appreciated by and alternatively in some ways caused friction with this other office, insights I would have never gained in a formal office setting.

There is a saying that goes "more business is done on the golf course than in the boardroom." There is a lot of truth in this. I do not play golf often and therefore I am not very good at it. I do golf occasionally, though, and the camaraderie you build on the course carries over into the office. This is especially useful if you play with people from outside your immediate office or work team. The knowledge and perspective you can gain can be invaluable because you can get a glimpse of what people are really thinking when they drop the professional mask, and you have longer conversations than you would simply passing in the hallway or making pleasantries while waiting for meetings to start. In this case, golf and SCUBA diving are merely examples. What are the social physical activities that you engage in and can use to help you build your network and influence?

Lunch is another time when you can build relationships and gain insights. I know a lot of people who either take lunch by themselves in the office or skip it to go to the gym or for a run on their own. They want to get away from people, or they are so busy (or want to appear so busy) that taking a lunch break will make them feel further behind. I always tried to make it down to the cafeteria for lunch, and I always tried to sit with a mixed group of people who were not from my own office. I am not trying to snub the people in my office. In fact, we usually offset our lunch times anyway, and we had a very collegial relationship, in and out of the office. What I am trying to do is build and maintain relationships with other offices and teams.

Lunch is a great place to gain insights and get up to speed on the latest events. There are often conversations that start with, "Hey, did you hear about..." While some of these conversations may be simple gossip or conjecture, other times there is serious discussion about important topics, and you can get some pretty unvarnished views from people. Knowledge of the projects in other departments may help shape the projects you are working on, and the collegial, collaborative relationships you build over a meal can have an important impact. Basically, RONI.

When you are leading an organization, it is even more important to show up. In my mid-level 2 assignment, each year my office served Christmas Eve and New Year's Eve dinner to the people who were stuck working. Yep, Christmas Eve at 6:50 p.m. each year for three years, I left whatever family festivities I was engaged in to go help serve dinner. Same thing on New Year's Eve. Why? Because I wanted to show my appreciation for the people who worked for me who were stuck working on the holiday. This activity had such a positive impact that it was something I looked forward to, instead of seeing it as a burden. I even took my six-year-old son with me, so he could experience the feeling of serving others, in this case literally serving them dinner.

When my office got together to celebrate someone's birthday or another social occasion, I made sure to be there, to show my appreciation for the staff and celebrate with them. When they lost a family member, I tried to make sure that I was at the wake or the funeral. I can't always make it; sometime life interferes, but I can always make sure to make a personal call on the grieving party to offer them my condolences.

In Chapter 13, I wrote about the awards process. Awards are important and so is showing up for awards ceremonies. I have had two supervisors who never go to awards ceremonies, not even to pick up their own awards. Further, they do not bother to go to ceremonies at which the people who work for them are being honored, even if they themselves wrote the nomination. This strikes me as so wrong. I had another supervisor who always went to the awards ceremonies, whether he or anyone else in the office was receiving something. I learned a lot about the value of attending these ceremonies from him.

First, if you are receiving an award, show up and accept it; otherwise, you are disrespecting the nominator. Second, if you are a supervisor who nominated someone in your work unit for an award, show up to complete that circle of honoring their accomplishment. Third, if someone in your work unit is receiving an award that someone else nominated them for, show up to honor the accomplishment and the nominator. Finally, even if there is no one in your work unit receiving an award at that ceremony, there are colleagues in other offices who probably are, so honor them.

In addition to honoring the people receiving the awards or those who wrote the nominations, attending awards ceremonies has a couple of other advantages. They are a great networking opportunity: awards ceremonies often bring together a large cross section of the organization, and it gives you a chance to interact with people from other divisions you might not see often. Also, feel free to be inspired by the awards. Did someone receive an award for a similar project you are developing, or does it spark an idea for a new project? Is there someone in your team who is doing something like someone who got an award? You can use this information to renew energy for a project, inspire your team, and even help ensure that you properly honor your own employees.

Now, as you have read this chapter, you may be thinking to yourself that what I am talking about is all about working an angle or gaining some leverage that you can use to your advantage. That is not the point. If that is your goal, it will soon be apparent to others, and instead of building relationships and opening collaborative opportunities, you will instead alienate these people you need. There is a great TEDx talk about this by my friend Daniel Hallak entitled, "Networking Does Not Have to Feel Gross" (Hallak, 2018).

In his talk, Hallak focuses on the importance of networking and building social capital, rather than trying to simply build transactional networks. He cites research and studies that show "Building social capital leads to a host of positive outcomes: job performance, salary levels, employability and so much more." But, he explains, "When people built relationships for selfish gain, it left them feeling dirty. And when they felt dirty, they were even less likely to engage with those people and to build those relationships. Even though that might be exactly what they needed for their success in their careers."

To build good networks, Hallak recommends switching the transactional question. Instead of focusing on what you can get from a contact, focus on what you can give them. Move from being a "greedy transactional consumer to being a generous relational investor." There is that word again, investor. Investing in relationships is important as a leader, and it is not hard. You just need to have the right mindset.

What this is really about comes back to the values that I talked about in Chapter 2: being friendly, courteous, and kind. It also has a lot to do with taking care of your pack as an alpha, as I mentioned in Chapter 9. You need to give to these relationships, not just take from them. If you do these things, people will notice: your subordinates, your peers, and people higher up the pyramid. It will increase your credibility and grow your leadership profile.

Showing up, even if you don't really feel like it, will raise your leadership meter and increase your influence. If you fail to show up, they are going to follow someone else who did. Make sure you build your network and foster a good RONI.

Here is the lesson:
To lead, you need to show up. Not just to your job, but also to the social functions and activities that are part of life outside the office walls. By showing up, you build and maintain relationships and gain knowledge. Don't just try to work the angles and gain leverage; be sincere and offer to give as much as you take from relationships.

REFERENCE

Hallak, D. (2018, April). *Networking doesn't have to feel gross* [Video]. TEDx Talks.   www.ted.com/talks/daniel_hallak_networking_doesn_t_have_to_feel_gross/transcript

Chapter 20

Simple encouragement

Smile and wave

It is amazing to me the effect that the simple act of smiling and waving can have on an organization. As I mentioned in Chapter 3, I am lousy with names. Partly, this is because I am a bit of an introvert, and partly, try as I might to correct it, I get stuck in my own head and ideas as I work to riddle out whatever problem or thoughts and mental connections I am chasing down.

What I have found, though, is that while remembering names is important and useful, recognizing people and interacting with them on a personal basis is even more useful. Recognizing people when you pass them in the hall, encounter them in the coffee shop, or see them hard at work can go miles in boosting morale and making people feel appreciated. And all it really takes is a smile and a wave. The higher up the bureaucratic food chain you are, the further this behavior will take you.

I was riding in a car with a supervisor once and as we passed one of our employees, he honked his horn, made eye contact with the employee, smiled, and waved. It was a simple, quick, limited interaction, but the smile in return was genuine. The boss had recognized the employee, and the employee felt proud.

There was a great saying I heard once, and while I cannot find the source, it really brings this concept home: "Encouragement is never small when you are on the receiving end of it." For you, a smile and a wave, or a word of recognition as you walk by may seem like an incredibly small thing, but you have no idea the effect it can have on the person receiving it. I have been on both sides of this, giving and receiving.

At one point in my mid-level 1 assignment, I was dealing with a really stressful project. I was annoyed with how part of it was progressing, and it showed on my face and in my body language. As I stalked through the halls, fuming, the ambassador saw me coming and simply said, "I really appreciate all of the work you are putting in to make this project a success." Did she know what it was I was actually working on? Probably not, but she did

DOI: 10.1201/9781003650454-24

understand that a lot of us were under tremendous pressure to make sure everything went smoothly.

Her words made some of the stress and strain melt away; not all of it, but the load was lightened a little. I was so shocked that all I could do was say, "thank you." The feeling, though, was profound, and as her words sank in, I realized that even if the particular piece bothering me was frustrating, it would work itself out and the overall project was in fact going very well. My mood brightened, and I was able to get a better perspective on the problem I was working on and to find a solution, just because of a few kind words of the person in charge.

On the flip side of this, in that same assignment I had a sizable team that I had oversight of, including the local guards that I mentioned earlier. Each morning, as I would walk in, I would smile and wave at each of the guards, ask how the equipment (metal detectors, X-ray machines, etc.) was working, and engage in a few pleasantries and ask how their families were doing. Literally, I was just passing through, trying to be friendly and show some interest in these people who worked for me. I had no idea the impact this was having.

This took no more than 60–90 seconds each morning, but the feedback I got from this group's direct supervisors was astounding. Through this simple act, morale increased, employee pride increased, and attention to duty increased. The supervisors told me that the employees felt truly appreciated. As I got ready to rotate, I was truly humbled when the employees pooled their limited resources, bought me a parting gift, and had me join them for a meal.

Smiling and waving can work on both small and large scales. When President Obama came to visit our worksite, the worksite held a "meet and greet." This is common when senior officials visit a worksite. President Obama arrived, said a few words, and shook a few hands. For most of the people present, though, all they got was a smile and a wave, but it was enough for them. All the work they had done to prepare for the visit suddenly felt appreciated.

You don't need to be the president or CEO to have this kind of impact, though. You can have this kind of impact in your own organization. I was waiting for a conference to start once at my agency headquarters, and as I sat at the table, the director of my agency walked through the room, saying hello and shaking hands with a couple of people, including me. The guy sitting next to me turned and said, "wow, you know the big boss." It made me feel good, it made me feel important; all it had been was a hello and a handshake.

This works even at lower levels. As I said, I was a mid-level bureaucrat. This means that I had people who worked for me, and there were people who worked for them. I was in the middle of the pyramid, but when I smiled and waved at the guards, made small talk with them as I paseds by, or spent a few minutes with other members of the team, it had much the same impact on them as it had on me when my boss's boss noticed me or my work.

I was intrigued enough with this concept that I started a little experiment. I spent a week making sure that every time I passed by one of my subordinates, or one of their subordinates, I took the opportunity to simply smile, wave, and ask, "Everything okay, do you need anything?" It was amazing the difference this made. By the end of the second day, people who typically were lost in their work, or carried stern expressions as they walked the building visibly brightened as I approached. They opened up and were friendlier not just to me but also to others. Their own courteousness to others increased, and the overall mood seemed to improve.

Since I engaged in this experiment and saw the results, I continued doing these things. No, I am not perfect at it; sometimes I am too absorbed in my own thoughts to remember to look at the guard in the window or at employee in the cubicle as I pass by, but that is now the exception rather than the rule. I also recently learned more about why this works, which I think is important to understand.

There has been quite a bit of research done on the power of encouragement and the "magic ratio" of encouragement to criticism, This includes a recent article by Arthur Brooks in *The Atlantic* that highlights research showing that high-performing teams typically have between five and six encouragements or compliments to every criticism, and for the lowest performing, this ratio is reversed, with between two and three criticisms for every encouragement. (Brooks, 2024).

Brooks also emphasizes that the compliments or encouragements need to be sincere. This was also reflected in my experience with The Kindness Games that I mentioned in Chapter 2. Praise does not need to be a big boisterous event. It can be as simple as an acknowledgment of a job well done, a simple smile and a wave, but it needs to be sincere.

Unfortunately, a lot of workplaces seem to have that ratio reversed and give five (or more) criticisms for each statement of praise. How many times have you had a paper or a proposal that you have written returned to you, covered in red ink with the simple instruction "fix this" (or some other unhelpful suggestion) notated at the top? How many times has the boss returned your report with a simple "good job" at the top?

All too often, there is the concept that people are supposed to "do their jobs" and that they should not need any encouragement to do them. A paycheck is enough. The feeling of service is enough. The feeling of a job well done is enough. Well, if you don't tell them that they are doing a good job, how do they get that feeling?

My supervisor in my mid-level 1 assignment had this attitude. He specifically instructed my colleagues and me, as his subordinate supervisors, that we were "not there to hold the employees' hands" and that "the employees are supposedly professionals and should be able to do their job without needing encouragement." He felt that if an employee needed encouragement to be able to give their best, they should go somewhere else.

This is what a lot of people did. They got out as quickly as they could, often leaving the office shorthanded. It was not that this supervisor handed out a lot of criticism, but he failed to realize the need to encourage, so the ratio was out of balance.

In one of my leadership training courses, we learned a technique to use when discussing areas for improvement. Areas for improvement are criticisms. There is no other way to slice it. When you criticize someone, they tend to get defensive. In the course, they explained that the goal for effectively communicating an area needing improvement is to couch it in terms of something the employee does well. Try to get the ratio right and focus on positive things the employee does, get the conversation flowing and get the employee engaged, and then shift into the area for improvement. This is referred to as a "criticism sandwich."

I have tried this approach and had mixed results. Sometimes, the employees were really open to criticism and able to discuss the matter without getting defensive. Occasionally, the conversation simply hits a brick wall, going along smoothly during the praise, completely shutting down when you mention an area for improvement. On the other hand, if there is no praise at all and the overall atmosphere is toxic to begin with, then the conversation will begin with defensiveness and go downhill from there.

Research shows that this advice to offer a criticism sandwich is flawed. According to an article by Steve Lowisz published in *Forbes*, this can often come across as insincere and undermine trust (Lowisz, 2022). Another article by Roger Schwarz that appeared in *Harvard Business Review* explains that using a transparent strategy based on honesty and mutual respect is much more effective (Schwarz, 2013). That trust and respect must be built over time. It starts with the little interactions that show you acknowledge and appreciate your team.

So, lighten the atmosphere in general, smile and wave, pay a compliment, say hello, give congratulations, be friendly, courteous, and kind. Getting the ratio right in the first place will go a long way toward creating an atmosphere to get the best results.

Here is the lesson:
Employees need encouragement. Studies have shown that having a
ratio of five encouragements to one criticism can have a profound

impact on the quality and level of productivity. Encouragement is never small when you are on the receiving end. A simple smile and a wave from you, the manager-leader, can show that you recognize the employees and the work they are doing, thereby moving the ratio in the right direction.

REFERENCES

Brooks, A. C. (2024, August 15). *A compliment that really means something.* The Atlantic. www.theatlantic.com/ideas/archive/2024/08/give-great-compliment-happiness/679447/

Lowisz, S. (2022, April 25). *Why the "sandwich" approach to criticism is terrible advice.* Forbes. www.forbes.com/sites/forbeshumanresourcescouncil/2022/04/25/why-the-sandwich-approach-to-criticism-is-terrible-advice/

Schwarz, R. (2013, April 19). *The "sandwich approach" undermines your feedback.* Harvard Business Review. https://hbr.org/2013/04/the-sandwich-approach-undermin

Chapter 21

Roadblocks

What if the managing supervisor is the problem?

In Part 2, I touched a couple of times on dealing with problem employees. But what if the problem employee is responsible for supervising others? From an organizational perspective, the problem can become touchier and more pronounced.

As a leader, you want to show your faith in your personnel by allowing them to run their organizational units. You give directions to the subordinate supervisor, those directions get carried out: you give the what, they figure out the how. They staff out the project as they see fit, because they are leaders (hopefully) and managers in their own right. If there is a discipline problem, they will take care of it and raise it to your level when necessary. You each have positional influence.

If there is a conflict between sections, and the section supervisors cannot address it, then it makes sense for you to step in, get the viewpoints of both sides, and make necessary decisions: you are ensuring your pyramid is balanced and not in danger of toppling over.

The question becomes: at what point do you step in when there are conflicts WITHIN a section?

The first step is PAYING ATTENTION. Often a supervisor with problems in their section does not want management to be aware of the issues, so the supervisor may try to address the problems themselves and keep the issue within their sub-pyramid. Only through paying close attention to the activities of the various sections will you be able to pick up on minor issues before they become major problems. You cannot influence what you do not know about.

In April 2011, Southwest Airlines had a problem in which the aluminum panels of one of its jets simply ripped off. This led to a catastrophic decompression and emergency landing. Luckily, only two people were hurt, both with minor injuries. The National Transportation Safety Board (NTSB), in reviewing the incident, found that blue paint had seeped between the panels that were riveted together. The NTSB found that constant strain on the system had led to metal fatigue, occurring much more quickly

DOI: 10.1201/9781003650454-25

than anticipated, causing the rivets simply to let loose. The NTSB report stated, "The hole quality in the crown and left side skin panels was not in accordance with Boeing specifications or standard manufacturing practices and showed a lack of attention to detail and extremely poor manufacturing technique" (National Transportation Safety Board, 2013). Had proper inspections been conducted, this problem could have been revealed before it became catastrophic.

So, what does this have to do with leadership? In this instance, a failure of leadership allowed the lack of attention to detail and poor technique. As a leader, you need to pay attention to the performance of your team. You need to watch for cracks and irregularities.

If deadlines are missed or barely met, it may be an indication of a bigger problem. If relationships appear to be getting stretched or frayed, it may be an indication of a bigger problem. The beauty of the pyramid within the pyramid organizational design of a good bureaucracy is that, as a leader, you have the ability, and responsibility, to reach down not only into the immediate pyramid you are in, but also into the sub-pyramids that make up your pyramid.

Second, let the supervisor know you are there to support them and use your influence to lead them. Mentor and coach them. Show that you recognize the problem and you understand they may be engaging in efforts to resolve it. Delve into the problem, asking questions about the issue and the solution the supervisor intends to implement. This may give the supervisor a feeling of support while allowing you to ensure the problem has not grown out of control and that the supervisor is not planning a solution that will exacerbate the situation. Of course, you need to make sure you have built a collaborative relationship with the subordinate supervisors to have the trust, mutual respect, and influence needed to accomplish this.

Follow up with the supervisor and ensure that the problem is being resolved. Unless and until it is necessary, you should not undermine the supervisor's authority and responsibility by forcing a solution. Doing so violates trust and undermines influence. At the same time, you need to maintain trust and influence with the rest of the team, so if there is no progress after a reasonable attempt to help the supervisor, or if the problem is getting substantially worse, intervene directly. Yes, it is a paradox.

Now, imagine a slightly different scenario: a section is performing at a high level and the members of the section are well liked and respected, but the supervisor is not, either by his section or his peers at the worksite. You may remember my mentioning Peter, one of my supervisors from my mid-level 2 assignment. It was not that Peter was incapable; he had great experience and was very smart. But he was lazy, and selfish.

Some people believe that once they achieve a certain level of management and authority, they can simply sit back, relax, and let the employees they supervise do the work. They believe that, as the manager, they are there to "supervise, not actually work."

Peter was very much like this. Reports awaiting his review would sit on his desk for weeks before he got around to them. The hours he kept were more than a little questionable: coming in late, leaving early, taking long coffee breaks and long lunches. He was often the butt of jokes by other managers at our worksite, but his section performed well, even though we were frustrated by Peter's lack of leadership and the poor example he set.

So, what to do in a situation like this? Remember, if you are managing an organization, step one is to pay attention, and step two is to take action to address the problem. If you recognize that an employee might be having a problem, and you fail to address it, then you are failing as leader. As a leader, you should try to use your influence to provide direction and improve the situation. But when your own supervisor is the problem, and their supervisor is not paying attention, things get more complicated.

In the example I related above, I had several opportunities to possibly address the problem with Peter's supervisor. Let's call the higher-level supervisor George. Occasionally, Peter was out of town, and I would deal directly with George.

I was really frustrated with Peter, as were other members of the team I was leading. I was doing my best to act as a buffer between Peter and the rest of the team, but it was exhausting. I strongly considered filing an official complaint, but I was counseled by a mentor to take a softer approach, to try to influence the situation in other ways instead.

This mentor, who was aware of the problems, believed it might backfire, and I would face retribution from Peter if I brought up the problems unasked. But if George asked how the section was doing, my mentor said I should be honest and not simply gloss over the issues.

I took this advice and hoped and prayed George would bring it up in one of our meetings. I was hoping he would notice that the level of productivity was higher when Peter was gone. Yet George never noticed and never asked; he was completely oblivious. His management style was one of "supervisors manage their sections, and if there is a problem in the section, the supervisor is responsible for taking care of it." What George missed was that because this bureaucracy is pyramids built on pyramids, he was the one responsible for addressing issues caused when supervisors below him were problematic.

Interestingly, I finally did offer George some insight into the issues affecting my office and some advice on how to constructively approach the issues. I was getting ready to rotate out of my job and on to another. As is a pretty standard practice, I had a final meeting with George, an outbriefing where we could say goodbye to each other and George could give me a "pep talk" for my upcoming assignment. In diplomatic parlance, this is a courtesy call (albeit a departure, rather than the traditional arrival courtesy call). George was extolling Peter's virtues, widely praising him and voicing his hopes for Peter's promotion.

I finally couldn't take it anymore. I said, "Well, actually, while Peter may have some good experience and may ensure that he always makes himself look good to you, those of us in the office are really frustrated with him," and outlined several examples.

I then offered some ways in which George could help with these problems, starting with asking him to pay a bit more attention to the section. I also suggested he might want to take action by counseling Peter on his leadership style and work habits. Finally, I offered some solutions to make improvements. For example, when Peter said he was going to a meeting with local contacts, George could ask which other staff member Peter was taking along to give them experience and exposure. Every so often, George could ask for an overview of what the employees in the sections were working on, or when a report was forwarded for review, he could ask Peter who actually wrote it so they could get the credit.

I cannot say for sure that my attempt to influence George was effective, but I heard from some of those I left and from my replacement that things did indeed get better. I just wish it had not taken so long for George to pay attention to the problem, or that I had been able to garner more influence in the situation to correct it earlier.

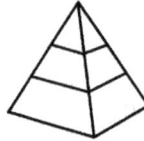

Here is the lesson:
If you supervise other supervisors, you are responsible not just for
your level of the pyramid, but the levels of the pyramid below you.
Pay attention, ask questions, and monitor the health and product-
ivity of the subsections. It may seem the section is running very
efficiently on the surface, but underlying frustrations and hidden
stressors may be causing damage that you will not see if you only
look at the section head and take him at his word that all is well and
wonderful.

REFERENCE

National Transportation Safety Board. (2013). *Accident Number: DCA11 MA039 (Report)*. www.ntsb.gov/investigations/AccidentReports/Reports/AAB1302.pdf

Chapter 22

Having an impact

Lead well and not only will people follow you, but they will name their children after you

As I explained in the introduction to this book, my Journeyman 1 position was in Africa. As part of that position, I oversaw a guard force that was made up of people on personal services contracts. This means that they did not work for a third-party vendor, as was fairly typical, but each had been individually hired by the embassy. Part of my role was to directly lead and manage this team.

When I arrived, the guard force was seriously undermanned, overworked, and had not had a raise in two years. A janitor working 40 hours a week made more on an annual basis than a guard working 60 hours a week. One thing the guards had going for themselves, though, was pride in their positions. There is a reason that Burkina Faso translates from the local languages (Mooré and Dioula), into "Land of the Upright People" in English. I worked hard to build on that sense of pride that the guard force already had, to nourish and nurture it.

I had three major goals regarding the guard force: implement a new training regimen, adjust their workweek to a more reasonable schedule, and bring their pay more in line with that of the rest of the employees. As I said, the guards had a lot of pride in their positions, but they felt overlooked. Part of that was due to the structure of the society in the country. Guards are generally looked at simply as watchmen: they are unarmed and stay in one place all day, and they aren't really seen as doing anything. While that may be true for many of the guards throughout the country, the guards working for me had a much higher level of responsibility, especially after 9/11.

In the aftermath of 9/11, we had no idea where the next attack would take place, and there were always rumors that more were being planned. We knew that embassies would always be a target, and in fact, the bombings of the US embassies in Nairobi, Kenya, and Dar es Salaam, Tanzania, in 1998 had been a wake-up call that even in countries considered safe, there was cause for concern.

The first line of defense, from recognizing an attack is being planned, to intercepting it and providing a response in the aftermath, is the local

DOI: 10.1201/9781003650454-26

guard force. Additionally, these guards were responsible for the operation of X-ray machines, metal detectors, camera systems, alarm systems, and a host of other security apparatuses. These guards were not simple watchmen, and they needed the skills to go along with their responsibilities.

I evaluated my guard force and then worked to implement a three-phase training plan: initial training for new guards, refresher training for guards currently on the job, and in-service training for everyone. The guards relished the opportunity to learn and were so grateful that someone had taken the time to work with them to help them improve. I received many comments from the other personnel at the embassy about the improved attentiveness and morale of the guard force.

As I implemented the training plan, I also worked to expand the size of the guard force. After 9/11, we added new guard posts, so we needed to increase the number of personnel to staff them. Also, I recognized that the guards were working 12 hours a day, six days a week, with no breaks for meals. They were constantly rotating between day shift and night shift, which was another serious problem. For one thing, they were exhausted; they were overworked and they could never adjust to a sleeping pattern before rotating shifts again. Also, because they were forced to eat their meals while on post, they were distracted from their duties.

While I could not expand the guard force enough to go to eight-hour shifts, I was able to reduce their workload to five days a week and hire enough guards to give each guard two one-hour breaks, one designated as a meal break, and the other designated as a training break. I also worked with the guard force to set up permanent shifts with the option to rotate between day and night shifts every three months (instead of every two days). These changes helped increase the guards' attentiveness and reduce fatigue, while allowing them to continue to sharpen their skills during the training breaks.

Finally, I worked with the budget office to raise the salaries of the guards. I did this in two ways. First, I worked for an outright increase. The rest of the embassy workforce had been given increases each of the two previous years, but because the pay of guards (watchmen) nationwide was so low, the guard force at the embassy was already among the highest-paid guards in the country, so their pay was frozen both years. I successfully argued that comparing our guard force to the local watchmen was insufficient due to the reasons I laid out above. The second thing I did was that when we changed the schedule, adding breaks and a second day off, I worked to ensure that the guard's annual salary remained at the newly raised level, even though they were working fewer hours in a year.

I did a few other things, as well, such as implementing a "guard of the month" program with a small cash award (only $50, but it meant a lot to them). I used the regular awards process to nominate guards for embassy-wide awards. This allowed the rest of the embassy staff to get a better sense of the work the guards were doing and how it helped keep the entire mission safe, raising the respect and appreciation for the guards across the wider mission.

I held monthly meetings of the guard force to review the progress we were making and take questions from them. I held receptions to celebrate the completion of the basic training for each group of new guards (yep, I paid for these out of my own pocket). I created a guard force command staff with a chain of command and opened promotion opportunities, providing them with additional training in administration and leadership.

My wife and I held a retirement ceremony and reception at our home for one of the senior guards, showing him honor for his service and contributions to our mission. This was also important because not only was he a senior guard, but he was a village elder, and showing him this respect was very important in the local culture. It was also simply the right thing to do as he had more than 20 years of service to our community.

As I prepared to leave, I held a meeting of the guard force to bid them farewell. A number of the guards and my other staff gave me personal tokens of affection. It was a very emotional scene because of the mutual care and respect we had developed for each other. In one particularly moving tribute, one of the guards announced that his wife was pregnant and that they had chosen to name their child after me because of everything I had done to improve their lives and increase the respect they had for themselves and from the community.

Lead well, and not only will people follow you, but they will also name their children after you.

I have had other experiences with this kind of personal devotion. Shortly after I left Africa for my onward assignment, I learned that one of the key staff members I had hired (the one who replaced the alpha I discussed in Chapter 9) had tendered his resignation within days after my departure. It turned out that several months earlier, he had been offered a much better job with a significant promotion by his previous employer, but he did not want to leave until after I had gone, out of respect for me and the efforts I had made to develop him as an employee and leader.

Also, as I concluded my mid-level 2 assignment, in addition to the kind words people had for me that I mentioned in the introduction, a number of staff from throughout the embassy broke down in tears because, as they expressed it, they thought so much of me as a leader, which is ironic given how much I struggled under Peter's "supervision."

I do not want to suggest that I am some kind of saint or miracle worker. I do not relate these stories in order to inflate my own ego. I share these with you because, like you, I do the best I can. I try to make a personal connection with the people I work with. I try to hold a bold, yet achievable vision of what I want to accomplish when I come into a new assignment and then I try to help the staff achieve that vision. I try to develop and manage my staff at all levels to give them opportunities for personal and professional growth. These lessons are tried and tested, and will perhaps give you ideas or insights into your own leadership journey.

To be sure, I am not perfect. Sometimes I am not paying attention to everything I should. Sometimes I have experiences that shock me back and make me realize I have slipped from my leadership path, and sometimes I see examples that I wish I could model but I lack the energy. Sometimes my models are above me; sometimes they are people I supervise.

In my mid-level 2 assignment, there was a man under my supervision who was the model of the personal leader. He was able to make personal connections with the people working for him like no one else I had ever seen. He had more energy and worked more deeply on more projects than I ever thought possible. He was truly a leader, mentoring his colleagues in how he operated, to help them achieve the same successes he enjoyed. While he worked for me in that assignment, I would not be surprised if someday, I will be working for him. And I would not be surprised if there are a number of children out there named for him due to the impact he had in their parents lives.

Here is the lesson:
Organizations are made up of people. If you want to lead an organ-
ization, you need to get the people to follow you. This means making
the people understand that you care about them and getting them
to believe in, respect, and care for you. This becomes a mutually
reinforcing cycle that strengthens both the organization and you as
the leader.

Chapter 23

Staying motivated

Starting is easy, finishing is another story

Leadership is a process; it is not a quick, one-off event. It takes work, and a lot of it, to be a proper leader. Education is not enough; it takes experience. Even when you think you have it down, that you have learned all of the lessons, there is always room to learn and grow. Also, you never know when a change will come that will cause you to need to rebuild your leadership credentials, standing, and capabilities.

As I reflect on more senior people I know who are in positional leadership posts, there are three traps that I see many otherwise excellent leaders fall into. I call them the three C's: Coasting, Cockiness, and Conservatism.

Coasting happens when you achieve a certain desired level and then decide that since you have made that level, it is time to simply sit back and enjoy the ride. Instead of really leading and being involved in operations, you simply staff things out.

There is a huge difference between effective delegating and "pigeon management," whereby you simply hover over someone's desk, drop something on it, squawk, and then fly off again, never bothering to check the results. Effective delegation involves employee development and empowerment, ensuring that the proper tasks are given to the right people and that you solicit feedback, and working with the delegate to ensure they have the tools they need to accomplish the task. Pigeon management is just crapping something out at whoever happens to be underneath you at the moment.

Leaders who turn into coasters also often suffer from an inability to share the spotlight (see Chapter 14). They still want to be seen as the leader and the one in charge (they have achieved this position of prominence after all), so they ensure that they get the credit for everything the work unit accomplishes. An otherwise good leader who turns into a coaster can be rehabilitated, but it will take a higher level of leadership to recognize the problem, and then address it. Having a set of mentors or coaches at more advanced levels is one way to help a leader avoid falling into this trap. Another way is to get the necessary feedback from people you lead and supervise, like the 360 model I discussed in Chapter 7.

Cockiness is another problem altogether. In June 2010, General Stanley McChrystal was profiled for *Rolling Stone* magazine. In the article, his senior staff voiced some opinions attributed to him that caused concern on the part of the higher levels of the chain of command (specifically the Joint Chiefs and the president). Very quickly he went from being General Stanley McChrystal, Commander of US Forces in Afghanistan (and on a path to going higher), to General Stanley McChrystal (retired).

During my excursion tour, I worked with a number of military personnel who had served under General McChrystal and they thought the world of him. He was innovative, an outstanding manager, a great thinker, and is rightly credited with a number of operational changes that helped reduce the levels of violence in Iraq and Afghanistan. He was a true leader that people were passionate about following. He was on the fast track up, and then his career fell off a cliff. While I cannot claim to know what he was thinking, from the outside, it looks like he got cocky; he forgot who he worked for and what his true place in the chain of command was. Luckily, he has managed to recover his mojo and has done great things teaching leadership and teamwork in the private sector. He has also been very forthright in taking responsibility for the incident that ended his career, absorbing the blame himself rather than trying to redirect it toward those around him (Martin, 2013). That is the mark of a true leader.

Frankly, I have had my own struggles with this. When I was in charge of emergency planning and working side-by-side with people way above my pay grade and experience level in my mid-level 1 position, I started to feel like I belonged with them. I forgot my true place in the pecking order. When I rotated jobs and had a manager who was firm on working a chain of command, I tripped over it several times and got counseled for violating it. It was a hard adjustment, and it still is.

I feel a lot like I never really settled into my mid-level 2 assignment because it was a deputy position, and I wanted to run my own office again. My frustration manifested as anger and ego more often than I realized. It affected my leadership of my team in my mid-level 3 assignment. Luckily, I had someone who was willing to confront me about it in a caring way. Also, in the mid-level 3 assignment, I had some fantastic role models above, alongside, and below me who were able to help me recover. It still took a long process to make that recovery lasting.

Again, a set of mentors who are willing to speak truthfully to you can be helpful in avoiding this trap.

Conservatism is the third trap. All leadership involves calculated risk. If the risk is not calculated, if you simply yell "yippee kay-yay" and throw caution to the wind, you are not going to get a lot of people to follow you down the road you have chosen. If, on the other hand, you are risk averse, you will be stagnant and no one will follow you because you are not going anywhere. So a leader takes calculated risks.

The problem becomes that as you advance in rank and climb up the pyramid, the view has a tendency to change. Maybe the risks you took as a mid-level manager seem foolhardy when you are a senior manager. Sure, they worked for you, but you attribute your success in the venture more to luck than to any wise path you chose. You then start to restrict the ability of the subordinate managers below you to take their own calculated risks. I am not saying that senior leaders do this because they are trying to consolidate their power. It may simply be that they have lost the connection with what it felt like to be a junior or mid-level manager. Or it may be that through their experience, they have a different view of the mistakes they made, or almost made, and want to prevent others from doing the same, especially if the consequences could be catastrophic.

I saw this growing risk aversion in several of the senior leaders with whom I rose through the ranks but who were promoted more quickly than me. They got where they were because they took calculated risks and made smart decisions. When they were near the top, though, their view had changed. They might still be taking calculated risks and making smart decisions for their level, but they were much more conservative in those risks. In my conversations with them, it was sometimes because they had more to lose personally. You do not want to draw the ire of Congress or the White House due to poor decision-making. It is a quick way to end a career. In other cases, simply the scope and scale of decisions could have serious, lasting, international consequences.

These individuals had also become more conservative in the risks they allowed their subordinates to take. The problem is a double-edged sword: their subordinate managers need the autonomy to take calculated risks, to be innovative, and to develop their own leadership portfolios, yet if they experience failure, not only will the subordinate managers need to answer for their failure (which is a part of growth as a leader), but the senior leaders will also be taken to task for allowing the risk in the first place. No one is better at creating blame for otherwise blameless situations than Congress and the media. How many excellent senior-level officials have been taken down simply because "there has to be someone to blame."

Finding the balance between reining your people in and letting them loose to do their best, even if they fail, can be hard. As things happen and small failures start to add up, or the microscope from above starts to bear down, the slide to risk aversion becomes more slippery. At its worst, it leads to gridlock because subordinate managers cannot make decisions without running everything up the chain. This is bureaucracy at its worst and is the antithesis of efficiency.

Solving risk aversion issues is probably the hardest. Recognizing the problem is the first step, though. When someone comes to you with an idea that seems risky, instead of rejecting it, pause to consider. What are the actual risks? What are the opportunities? What are the threats? What is the likely impact if the idea fails?

There has been a lot written about management risk in a variety of domains: financial, operational, security, cybersecurity, and so forth. Finding the balance between risk tolerance and risk appetite, or as Gav Schneider phrases it in his book *Presilience: How to Navigate Risk, Embrace Opportunity, and Build Resilience*, "Dynamic Risk Equilibrium" can be difficult (Schneider, 2025). It is a process in and of itself, difficult, but not impossible. Again, finding the right mentors, engaging in constant learning, and doing a lot of self-reflection can help you avoid this trap, increase efficiency, and return to high performance.

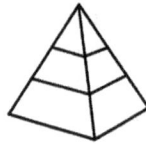

Here is the lesson:
To keep leading, you need to keep moving forward. As you achieve higher levels of leadership, you need to beware of the traps of the three C's: Coasting, Cockiness, and Conservatism. Any of these traps can be fatal to your leadership portfolio. Keep learning, keep working, keep leading, and people will continue to follow you.

REFERENCES

Martin, R. (Host). (2013, January 13). *"I accepted responsibility": McChrystal on his "share of the task"* [Audio interview transcript]. NPR. www.npr.org/2013/01/13/168966608/i-accepted-responsibility-mcchrystal-on-his-share-of-the-task

Schneider, G. (2025). *Presilience: How to navigate risk, embrace opportunity, and build resilience.* Amplify Publishing.

Chapter 24

Conclusion

Leadership is a process. It is not learned or accomplished quickly. It requires constant attention and refinement. First, you need to be able to lead yourself. This starts with understanding your own influences, role models, values, strengths, and weaknesses. You need to be aware of your limits and the importance of self-care. Focus on personal growth and continuous learning, because change is constant and you need to learn to be able to adapt. Finally, you need to know what impression you make on others, and how to manage it.

As you learn to lead yourself, you can begin to work on leading others. You do not have to wait until you have perfected your leadership of yourself. Frankly, you will never "perfect" it, because there is always something new to learn.

So as you begin to lead others, you need first to understand the difference between managing, supervising, and leading. Remember, you manage projects and programs. You supervise, and hopefully lead, people. You will need to learn the different motivations of those you hope to lead. You will need to learn to build alliances and identify who, like the alpha, you need to work with or around to form those alliances and take on a leadership role in a group. You must learn to enforce discipline and must gain the courage to deal with problematic employees or team members, rather than shirking the responsibility by "reprimanding all." You must earn credibility and operate with integrity. One way to do this for those you lead is to ensure that the rules you make are enforceable and sensible, and when you are confronted with rules imposed from above that do not meet that criteria, you must work to get them changed. Like a good Dungeon Master, you must work to develop those under your care and make sure you take steps to reward them properly through the awards process and through sharing the spotlight with them.

As you begin to lead others, look for ways to lead not just small groups but also entire organizations. Learn how to communicate up your bureaucratic pyramid. Learn how to craft and sell a vision, and how to build alliances to help you find the right decision-makers to put your vision into action. Understand the importance and methods of leading project teams and committees to influence the organization and accomplish your goals. Build your network and focus on your RONI—return on network investment—along with creating value for the networks of those you lead and support. Understand the power of simple encouragement to connect with people, and that encouragement is never small when you are on the receiving end of it. The influence and credibility you gain from "small encouragements" can be immeasurable in the context of a large organization.

As you begin to lead organizations, and especially as you move into positions of responsibility, make sure to pay attention to ensure the teams in the pyramids you oversee are functioning well. If there are supervisors who are failing to lead, you need to be enough of a leader to deal with the situation.

Organizations, just like small teams, are made of people. Make sure you care for the people in your organization. You cannot simply assume that people know you care for them if you lead from behind a desk. You need to get out and meet with them, spend time with them. Celebrate and mourn with them. As you show you care for the people in the organization, their care for you will increase. A very wise friend of mine is fond of saying, "no one will care about how much you know, until they know how much you care."

Finally, I begin where I started this conclusion. Leadership is a process. Beware of the three traps I outlined in Chapter 23: coasting, cockiness, and conservatism. Surround yourself with other leaders, mentors, and coaches. These should be people with whom you can be honest, and who will be honest with you.

This book does not contain an exhaustive list, nor do I claim that all of the lessons will apply to all levels of leadership, all leadership styles, or all situations. Leadership is a process; it is constantly evolving. You need to learn your own lessons. Hopefully, my stories and examples have helped you think of your own. One of the things that writing this book and reflecting on this topic has done for me is to show me how much more I need to learn and how far I need to go. It has also allowed me to dream bigger and recapture the optimism of my early career.

While this book focused on my experience and the lessons I learned in the first half of my career, I continued to learn more in the second half as I went from navigating the pyramid to climbing it. My goal in writing this volume is to help those who are starting out or those who are stuck to learn some of the key lessons that will help them develop their leadership skills.

As I detailed in Chapter 6, change is constant, even within the same organization. You need to keep making adjustments. You can always improve yourself, improve how you lead and interact with others, and ultimately that will improve how you lead organizations. I have included a list of resources in the appendix to help you continue on your leadership journey. Leadership is a process; it never stops. Let's go.

Appendix

Additional resources

While this book may serve as an introduction to your leadership journey, there are many resources out there that I encourage you to explore. With the exception of some of the books listed below these are in addition to the resources that are already referenced in the text.

Podcasts (available on various platforms)

These are leadership-oriented podcasts that I regularly follow and listen to (in alphabetical order, the descriptions are mine to help you choose which you may want to try out):

- **Coaching for Leaders with Dave Stachowiak** – Great content on leadership topics with a huge back library of episodes, a weekly guide, and additional content.
- **Coaching Real Leaders with Muriel Wilkinson** – Actual live coaching sessions with people working through their leadership development issues facilitated by a master coach.
- **HBR IdeaCast** – Great insights into business and leadership, helping you become a more well-rounded leader through understanding the view from different pyramids.
- **Leader Readycast by the National Preparedness Leadership Institute** – Conversations with emergency and crisis professionals to help you prepare for the "You're It" moments.
- **Leadership Tea Podcast: Sipping Wisdom, Stirring Success** with Shelby Smith-Wilson and Belinda Jackson-Farrier – Conversations between the hosts and their guests about leadership fundamentals and their experience.
- **The Craig Groeschel Leadership Podcast** – A Christian-based podcast focused on leadership development at all levels.

The **Great Conversation** with Ron Worman – An examination of various facets of business and leadership development, often focused on the security industry as Ron interviews his eclectic guests.

The **McKinsey Podcast** – An examination of business and leadership topics from one of the premier consulting companies.

The **One Thing** – Personal and leadership development conversations focused on helping you find strategies and paths to successes.

The **WiLD Conversation Podcast** – Whole and Intentional Leadership Development principles and insights with Dr. Rob McKenna and guests.

Online subscriptions

There are dozens of newsletters, daily mailers, blogs, and other such things you can subscribe to. Part of the problem is the sheer volume of all the material. There are a couple that I subscribe to that I look at frequently (and that are available for FREE!):

- Always Care Community – Paul Moxness on Substack
- Harvard Business Review Leadership Tips of the Day
- Mindfulness by Miles – From Miles Everson on LinkedIn.
- TED Talks Daily – I don't listen to all of them, but TED has some fantastic short-form content on a wide range of topics.
- Yes And! – Avish Parashar's Blog (improvisation, leadership, and inspiration)

Books

The following books are referenced in the text:

Aristotle. (1998). *Politics* (C. D. C. Reeve, Trans.). Hackett Publishing Company. (Original work published ca 350 bce)

Boy Scouts of America. (1990). *Boy Scout handbook* (10th ed.). Boy Scouts of America.

Brown, B. (2018). *Dare to lead: Brave work. Tough conversations. Whole hearts.* Random House.

Isaacson, W. (2014). *The innovators: How a group of hackers geniuses and geeks created the digital revolution.* Simon and Shuster.

Kouzes, J. M., & Posner, B. Z. (2023). *The leadership challenge* (7th ed.). Wiley.

Laney, M. O. (2002). The introvert advantage: how quiet people can thrive in an extrovert world. Workman.

Logan, D., King, J., & Fischer-Wright, H. (2008). *Tribal leadership: Leveraging natural groups to build a thriving organization.* Harper Business.

Maxwell, J. C. (1998). *The 21 irrefutable laws of leadership.* Thomas Nelson.

McKenna, R. (2017). *Composed: The art and science of leading under pressure.* Dustjacket Books.

Pink, D. H. (2009). *Drive: The surprising truth about what motivates us.* Riverhead Books.

Schneider, G. (2025). *Presilience: How to navigate risk, embrace opportunity, and build resilience.* Amplify Publishing.

In addition to the books referenced in the text, I draw inspiration and insights from histories and biographies (though action spy thrillers are my guilty pleasure and beach reads: you might be amazed at the number of leadership principles that can be gleaned from those as well). Walter Isaacson and David McCullough have written some excellent books, and these authors are able to weave amazing narratives based on their voluminous research into their subjects. Some examples that I keep on my bookshelf include:

By Walter Isaacson:

- *Benjamin Franklin: An American Life*
- *Einstein: His Life and Universe*
- *Leonardo da Vinci*
- *Steve Jobs*

By David McCullough

- *John Adams*
- *Mornings on Horseback* (Theodore Roosevelt)
- *The Wright Brothers*
- *Truman*

Other biographies and histories include:

- *Adams vs. Jefferson,* by John E. Ferling
- *Alexander Hamilton,* by Ron Chernow
- *Boyd: The Fighter Pilot Who Changed the Art of War,* by Robert Coram
- *John Marshall: Definer of a Nation,* by Jean Edward Smith
- *Lawrence in Arabia: War, Deceit, Imperial Folly and the Making of the Modern Middle East,* by Scott Anderson
- *The House of Morgan: An American Banking Dynasty and the Rise of Modern Finance,* by Ron Chernow
- *Unbroken: A World War II Story of Survival, Resilience, and Redemption,* by Laura Hillenbrand

Of course, I also read leadership and self-improvement books. Here are a few that I have found particularly useful:

- *Crisis Ready: Building an Invincible Brand in an Uncertain World*, by Melissa Agnes
- *Culture Rules: The Leader's Guide to Creating the Ultimate Competitive Advantage*, by Mark Miller
- *How to Develop Your Personal Mission Statement*, by Steven R. Covey
- *Range: Why Generalists Triumph in a Specialized World*, by David Epstein
- *Start with Why: How Great Leaders Inspire Everyone to Take Action*, by Simon Sinek
- *The Coaching Habit: Say Less, Ask More & Change the Way You Lead Forever*, by Michael Bungay Stanier
- *The Go-Giver: A Little Story about a Powerful Business Idea*, by Bob Burg and John David Mann
- *The ONE Thing: The Surprisingly Simple Truth about Extraordinary Results*, by Gary Keller and Jay Papasan
- *The 7 Habits of Highly Effective People*, by Stephen R. Covey
- *Tribe of Mentors: Short Life Advice from the Best in the World*, by Tim Ferris

Last, philosophy helps inform your leadership journey. Some of the ancient philosophers can be difficult to get through, but more modern translations make their works accessible.

- Aristotle – *Politics*
- Marcus Aurelius – *Meditations*
- Plato – *The Republic*
- Sun Tzu – *The Art of War*
- Thomas Hobbes – *The Leviathan*

As I said in the conclusion, leadership is a process. The above is by no means an exhaustive list of resources, but hopefully it gets you started or moves you forward in your leadership journey.

Index

For Product Safety Concerns and Information please contact our EU
representative GPSR@taylorandfrancis.com
Taylor & Francis Verlag GmbH, Kaufingerstraße 24, 80331 München, Germany